Praise for *Searching for Grace*

Searching for Grace invites you into the kind of relationship we all long for deep in our hearts. The relationship between Scotty and Russ is scary, vulnerable, and painful, but gorgeously loving and drenched in grace. The transparency of their relationship will frighten, disarm, and attract you all at the same time. But what is genius about this book is that the relationship between these two men is more than a model—it is an invitation to the only relationship that can heal you, profoundly reorder you, and restore to you the shalom that was shattered in the Garden, which has seemed so elusive ever since. Every conversation in this book reminds us that it is God and the healing grace that comes through his Son that we all long for. I know of no other book like this one.

PAUL DAVID TRIPP, author of *New Morning Mercies: A Daily Gospel Devotional*

Scotty and Russ's story of faith friendship welcomes us into a journey of vulnerability, honest questions, and the gift of being shaped by God's grace. These healing conversations give me hope that we will one day know in full what we only now see in part.

SANDRA MCCRACKEN, singer/songwriter

Consume this labor of love as precious wisdom. Even if you are not a pastor, read this book. I couldn't help but wonder what levels of hell I might have avoided if I'd have taken this in at a younger age. Scotty and Russ engage in a deeply honest, compelling, and life-changing conversation that we not only get to overhear but also partake in as co-laborers living out grace. This book will fortify you for your work, and far more for your joy in the gospel.

> **DAN B. ALLENDER**, Ph.D., professor of counseling psychology and founding president of The Seattle School of Theology and Psychology; author of *Healing the Wounded Heart* and *Leading with a Limp*

Searching for Grace echoes so much of what I've enjoyed in my friendship with Scotty through the years. The best mentoring happens when leaders own their brokenness and weakness and invite others into the welcome of God's grace and the freedom of his transforming love. Scotty and Russ chronicle their shared growth in grace and invite us to risk more honesty, vulnerability, and openness to God's pursuing heart.

> **LAURA STORY**, Grammy Award–winning artist

Years ago, feeling clueless and defeated and anxious and afraid, I picked up the phone and called the office of a highly esteemed pastor who didn't know me from Adam. Not only did Scotty Smith take the call and give me two full hours of his time, he also invited me to call him any time, and often. Since then, Scotty has been to me the most important kind of mentor—a shepherd of my heart in the grace I so often struggle to believe. After more than two decades of friendship, Scotty remains my gospel mentor. I am so thankful that younger ministers like Russ Masterson have also discovered the treasure that Scotty is.

For the joy of our souls, Scotty and Russ share their journey in grace together.

SCOTT SAULS, senior pastor of Christ Presbyterian Church in Nashville, Tennessee; author of several books, including *Jesus Outside the Lines* and *A Gentle Answer*

I've known Scotty for years, and every single time I talk to him, I feel seen, accepted, and loved. That's not because Scotty is so awesome but because the God who sees, accepts, and loves Scotty is so awesome. When we believe God loves us, we're free to love others. This book is a picture of Russ and Scotty's wonderful friendship—two men with plenty of pain and struggle in their lives, reminding one another (and us) of the great, inexhaustible love of the Father.

ANDREW PETERSON, singer/songwriter, author, and founder of the Rabbit Room

Where can we find peace? There's no formula, but thankfully Russ and Scotty show us how peace has found them, and continues to find them, in the restless flux of ordinary life. While never being prescriptive or burdensome, these two trustworthy guides narrate their experience with intimacy, candor, and grace, such that, by the time you put this book down, fear and burnout have dissipated and the reality of belovedness has burrowed into your heart afresh. Balm for the soul!

DAVID ZAHL, author of *Seculosity* and director of Mockingbird Ministries

searching for grace

A Weary Leader, a Wise Mentor,
and Seven Healing Conversations
for a Parched Soul

Scotty Smith
& Russ Masterson

TYNDALE
MOMENTUM®

The Tyndale nonfiction imprint

Visit Tyndale online at tyndale.com.

Visit Tyndale Momentum online at tyndalemomentum.com.

TYNDALE, Tyndale's quill logo, *Tyndale Momentum*, and the Tyndale Momentum logo are registered trademarks of Tyndale House Ministries. Tyndale Momentum is the nonfiction imprint of Tyndale House Publishers, Carol Stream, Illinois.

Cover designed by Koko Toyama

Interior designed by Mark Anthony Lane II

Edited by Stephanie Rische

Published in association with the literary agency of WordServe Literary Group, www. wordserveliterary.com.

For information about special discounts for bulk purchases, please contact Tyndale House Publishers at csresponse@tyndale.com, or call 1-800-323-9400.

ISBN 978-1-4964-4403-5

Printed in the United States of America

27	26	25	24	23	22	21
7	6	5	4	3	2	1

To Darlene, for forty-nine years of being my incredible wife, best friend, and partner-in-longing for the day of all things new and all things beautiful, and to Jack and Rose Marie Miller, for showing and telling me 97 percent of the things I know to be true about the gospel of God's grace.

SCOTTY

To my wife, Kristy, who continues to walk with me in tender and resolute grace.

RUSS

Contents

Foreword

SCOTTY AND RUSS'S BOOK is a new chapter in the story of God's relentless pursuit and fierce love that I've been living with my friend Scotty for nearly thirty-five years. When I look at the subtitle, I have to agree, because Scotty truly has been and continues to be a wise mentor in my life!

He's been that to many of us, precisely because he's been honest about his own seasons of overwhelming weariness and his parched-soul reality. That has freed me to do the same with Scotty. We've shared platforms, written two books, and fished some remarkable water together, but what has marked our relationship more than anything else is that we are two needy men who are so thankful God is the God of all grace.

Our friendship began at the intersection of our shared love for words, our thirsty hearts, and a new church Scotty had planted in Franklin, Tennessee. Christ Community Church was unique in many ways, but what captured my heart and the heart of my bride, Mary Beth, was the message of grace that we were hearing for the first time. I still remember driving home after a service one Sunday morning and hearing Mary Beth say as she shook her head, "If what Scotty is saying about God's grace is true, this really is Good News!"

Like many of our friends who ended up at the church, we came from more of a performance-based, do-more, try-harder version of the faith. There's no doubt we knew Jesus, but there was so much more to the gospel than we realized. (There still is . . . as I'm continuing to learn!) The gospel was being presented in ways that made Jesus the focus and the hero of the whole Bible.

Grace wasn't described as something, but as someone—Jesus himself. So many of Scotty's teachings and our conversations around them became the inspiration for songs that I've written and recorded over the years. "Magnificent Obsession," "God Is God," "Not Home Yet," "Dive," "Lord of the Dance" (which Scotty actually cowrote with me), "All Things New," "See the Glory," and "Speechless" are just a few of the songs that sprouted from the seeds of truth that God used Scotty to plant in my heart.

Scotty didn't preach like he was trying to fix anybody or to prove he was smarter or more right than others. It was obvious he was just as needy, hungry, and excited about what we were learning as anybody in the room, and that made what he was talking about all the more irresistible. People from all kinds of backgrounds crammed into an old sanctuary in downtown Franklin, with orangish pews and clashing orange shag carpet. It didn't matter.

All of us were, as Russ and Scotty's title says, searching for grace. But even more so, grace was searching for—and finding—us. That journey continues. Though I've yet to meet Russ, his questions and interactions with Scotty are so familiar. I got to walk with Scotty through many of the pain-unto-grace stories he shares in this book.

I'll add a story of my own to the mix. When I was writing and recording my album *Speechless*, Scotty began working on our first book, also titled *Speechless*. He called one day suggesting a subtitle that he was really excited about: *Living in Awe of God's Disruptive Grace*.

I had a ringside seat when God decided to make that subtitle a reality in Scotty's life. The record and book came out, and we hit the road in the summer of 1999 on a promotion tour. All went really well until we led a final event in downtown Cincinnati. It was for the great youth ministry organization Youth Specialties. By now, we could have done our presentation on cruise control. I shared a few songs off the *Speechless* record, then Scotty came out and shared a few thoughts about the wonders of God's grace.

But something about that afternoon was different. I finished my miniset, but when Scotty came to the mic, I could tell something was going on. My brother, whose words usually flow freely, was struggling. After finishing his seven minutes, which he later told me felt like seven hours, he closed with prayer and came off the stage. I asked him if he was okay, and he didn't really have much to say, which was unusual for him. This wasn't exhaustion. It was a work of God's Spirit and kindness.

Perhaps Scotty had been a bit prophetic with the phrase "disruptive grace." For the next few years, I watched my brother, friend, and pastor begin the healing journey that runs through much of this book. As Scotty puts it, God's grace will disrupt us before it delights us. Theoretical grace is only good for theoretical needs. Jesus has come to set actual prisoners free.

My friend's willingness to enter his burnout, process his heart wounds, get the help he needed, and start becoming a healthier man have graced the past twenty years of our friendship. These patterns have taken both of us deeper into the heart of God—at times gladly and at times reluctantly.

Scotty's vulnerability has helped me embrace mine. His stories and his journey of loss didn't make burying our daughter Maria any easier. But his fierce and faithful friendship has made me feel so much less alone and freer to risk bringing my anguish, anger, and fear to the throne of grace. Scotty and I continue to own our weakness together, because that's where the sweetness and aroma of grace are most likely to be found.

And we continue to dream, fish, play, ache, and serve Jesus together . . . longing for the day of all things new to get here, more confident than ever that it's actually coming!

Steven Curtis Chapman

Authors' Note

THIS BOOK GREW OUT of the mentoring relationship and conversations between Scotty and Russ. The book is primarily written in Russ's voice, with Scotty contributing his own narratives throughout. All writing by Scotty is entitled "From Scotty." Both authors played key roles in developing and editing the content of the entire book.

THE PORCH CONVERSATION

RUNNING ON EMPTY

How Did I Get Here?

My FIRST CONVERSATION with Scotty was on a long, narrow porch in the North Georgia mountains. The porch was filled with rocking chairs and swings and was attached to a barn. Men sat scattered around, talking about SEC football, theology, and the life they had retreated from to take in some rare moments of quiet.

Just inside was a two-story vaulted great room, a kitchen, and a hallway lined with several bedrooms. Beyond the living quarters was a simple structure with a dirt floor, filled with stalls, hay, and horses. Just thirty minutes before, I'd perched high in the loft of the barn listening to Scotty teach the group of men sitting in camp chairs and hammocks while a fresh breeze filled the loft from the outside twilight.

Fifty men had come here to sleep under the stars, to cast a fishing line or fire a gun, to listen and learn, to make a friend and share a conversation. I was there as one of the leaders, the pastor of twenty men attending from our young church. I was also there as a participant.

I was a thirty-five-year-old pastor attempting to keep my life under control.

Physically I was a whole person sitting in that barn, but my interior life was frazzled, and I was unsure if I could put myself together—or be put back together at all. Two questions were pulsing in me: *How did I get here?* and *How does this get better?*

Just a year earlier, I had started a church with a handful of people, hoping our small start-up would survive and make a difference in our community. Before that, I had been an associate pastor at a large church in Atlanta, and the departure from that haven of establishment and safety left me feeling exposed and anxious. As we moved out on our own, my wife and children were content and adjusting, but I was a mess inside.

That night, Scotty's words pierced my soul. He spoke of loss, avoidance, abuse, religious performance, and finally grace and peace. I had heard him speak once before, at a huge conference in southern Florida, where he stood onstage in front of thousands of people. Scotty was familiar with such settings: he had started and led a church in Nashville that grew to four thousand people. He'd written books and taught as an adjunct professor at several seminaries around the country. I had been sitting in the back of the room at that conference, and I never had the nerve to approach him. But now, at the retreat, I could sense a growing urgency in my spirit.

Scotty told us about coming out from behind the curtain of running, avoiding people, and performing for approval. The curtain had kept him from simply being *with* people. He said his life's theme song had been "Running on Empty" by Jackson Browne: "Running on empty, running blind."[1]

I knew the feeling.

Scotty said, "*Who we are* matters to God more than *what we do*. Our calling is to be worshipers, not workers; present, not impressive. Our truest identity is found in being God's beloved sons and daughters." Scotty bared his past and shared his present fears. He told the story of his own imperfection and how he now rests in the arc of God's story for him. He didn't speak as one perfect and completely healed but as one in the process of healing and growing in the awareness of the lavish love of God.

As I sat there looking out at the stars, I felt as if he had made a leap my soul knew I needed to make. This wasn't the first time I'd sensed this longing for a more abundant life. But it did feel like a calling into deeper waters.

Barbecue was served, and I watched as Scotty found a place on the porch. He had on brown leather Birkenstocks, gray hiking pants, and a casual, plaid button-down shirt with a zipped-up fleece vest. Even though he had just spoken of trauma and weakness—vulnerabilities that would have sent me into hiding for weeks—he comfortably shared a meal and chatted with guys about fly-fishing for trout.

As dinner concluded, I tossed my plate in the trash and waited nearby, hoping for a moment to begin a conversation. Scotty stood against the rail of the porch, his six-foot frame leaning slightly backward. I don't remember what I said, but I know my intention: *What does he know that I don't know yet?*

Scotty told me, almost a decade later, that I was "redemptively pestering him" on that porch. A year and a half passed after that conversation before I reached out to him with an email, asking if he would mentor me.

● ● ●

When I decided to start our church with my wife, Kristy, and two other couples, it felt like I might as well have been trying to start a mutual fund. I didn't know where to begin, nor did I know the steps to take after beginning. I immediately became overwhelmed by questions about bylaws, vision, values, financial accountability, caring for people, and leadership structures. Out of desperation, I began attending a monthly gathering in Atlanta led by experienced pastors who coached younger pastors about how to launch and lead a church. Through that gathering, I was paired with a pastor named Jake, and he became my coach as we formed our church of three families.

Jake was around fifty years old and was the founding pastor of a small bilingual church in a neighboring town. Jake held my hand as I raised support money for the first time in my life, formed a core group of parishioners, began a Bible study in the lobby of a dentist's office, and eventually launched a church with thirty adults and a herd of children in a preschool cafeteria.

Just eight months after our church launched, our community was shattered when a dear friend from our tight-knit group took his own life. The morning of the funeral, when I was still reeling from shock and grief, Jake showed up at my house, dressed in his finest suit. Without waiting for me to ask, he drove me to the funeral in his Honda Accord.

When I walked into the church, Jake was with me. When the sound tech helped me put on my microphone, Jake was with me. When I found the family and prayed with them, Jake was with me. When I sat quietly and prepared to officiate my first funeral, Jake was sitting beside me. When I stood in front of six hundred people and talked about my friend and the God who loves him, I looked out to my left, and Jake was right there, in the front row.

During this season our church was growing slowly and steadily. The ministries of teaching and caring for people were developing. As our numbers and ministries increased, the need for administrative processes increased too. Then we bought a building, which meant we needed to raise even more money to renovate it.

"Russ, you're beginning to ask me questions I don't know the answers to," Jake said to me as we sat in my home office above the garage. We could hear the laughter of my three girls and a few of their neighborhood friends from the backyard below.

"What do you mean?"

"You're asking me about organizational development, about running a building, and I haven't walked this path," Jake said.

"I understand." I nodded. "Okay."

Even as I said the words, I was sad for what this meant. The truth was, I'd noticed this trend over the past few months too. I would throw questions Jake's way, but he was unable to answer to the degree that satisfied either of us.

"It's time for you to find another coach," he said.

Where Can I Find Peace?

MONTHS PASSED after recognizing my need for a new coach. My questions and anxiety stacked up. I found myself unable to transform my heart and mind from anxiety and volatility to a place of peace. One Tuesday I yelled at the woman working at the post office, daydreamed the afternoon away, called the post office to apologize, and then came home in a general angst, harping on my young daughters who were creating a mess throughout our home.

Kristy dispensed grace to me. She was patient while I was emotionally erratic. We both knew something had to change. This wasn't just a bad day; this was a bad new normal. I needed more than a coach to help me lead our church; I needed a mentor to help me with the entirety of my life.

I emailed Scotty at a point when my anxiety was dismantling me. Asking Scotty to mentor me was a long shot at best; it was a half-court shot at the buzzer. But Scotty prayerfully considered my request and eventually said yes. I laid out our relationship plan like a long-distance bromance. We would video chat monthly for an hour and a half, we would visit each other often, and we would call and text without reservation.

I began to keep a special page in my journal reserved for questions for Scotty:

> *How are you present with someone when everything in you is swirling?*
> *What do you do when you feel like you're about to tip over?*
> *What do you say to a man who found out his wife is cheating on him?*
> *What do you say to a woman lying in hospice, about to die?*
> *How do you develop a fellowship structure for the church?*
> *Why am I so anxious? Were you anxious?*
> *What causes fear?*

I would ask these questions during our monthly conversations, and as Scotty and I talked, it was as if time stood still. These were holy moments for me. It was like growing up again—receiving an education in the grace and peace of God. By the end of our chats, Scotty always turned the tables and asked me questions.

> *How is your marriage?*
> *How are you doing as a dad?*
> *How is your soul?*
> *What would a healthier and freer you look like?*

I told Scotty the truth, not the half-truths I was accustomed to giving out, because I felt safe with him.

"A family is leaving our church," I told Scotty.

"Oh, I'm sorry," he said. "How does that make you feel?"

"It's just a disappointing thing. I mean, I know they should go to church wherever they want to. I want them to find the place that's right for them. But for some reason I'm still sort of upset."

"Feeling rejected is always hard. And it's sad to see friends leave. All of us react differently to feeling rejected or being disappointed. Our insecurity kicks in pretty quickly."

"What should I do?" I asked.

"Know that God loves you no matter what," he said. "Call them. Pursue them in love. Then send them away in love."

It occurred to me maybe the pain of having this family leave wasn't just about that particular situation but about an ongoing fear that ran in my heart about being second place, about being overlooked, about not being good enough. God was using Scotty's words to heal a wound I didn't even know was festering inside me. He was reminding me of something I needed to grasp about my true worth—not just as a pastor, but as a person.

His words were full of compassion rather than judgment. He offered a listening ear and passed on wisdom from his own experience, but he never gave me an "I'm going to fix you" lecture. He talked, and I took notes, and at the end of our conversations, he always told me he loved me. I don't remember the first time he said those powerful words, but I remember feeling like it was about five years too early for my guarded and resistant heart. I wondered if there was a "but" coming at the end of those words: "I love you, *but you need to . . .*" or "I love you, *but you should . . .*"

Scotty never put conditions on his love. So I started saying, "I love you" in return.

Ever so slowly, I was learning to give—and, with difficulty, learning to receive.

●   ●   ●

After Scotty and I had been talking for two months, I was taking a road trip with Kristy and my three daughters, ages two, four, and seven. We were headed from our home outside of Atlanta to my in-laws' in Orlando. As the highway stretched before me for seven hours, I found myself reflecting on the conversation Scotty and I had just had about peace and identity.

"I'm always on edge on the inside. I just want more peace," I said to Kristy—partly questioning and partly just musing out loud. "How can I be more secure in my belovedness—my identity as someone deeply loved by God?"

After talking for an hour, I noticed that Kristy wasn't responding anymore. I glanced over to the passenger seat and saw that her head was nodding about and she was fast asleep. I continued to contemplate the lessons inside my own head and heart. I found myself wishing my conversations with Scotty were recorded so I could go back to them, so I could share them directly with Kristy instead of constantly saying, "Well, you know, Scotty says . . ."

As I replayed Scotty's words in my head, I wondered, *Could I refine these lessons to the vital principles of grace that bring peace to a human soul?*

I wasn't sure, but it was worth a shot.

So after we talked the next time, I pulled out a little black journal and began jotting down the lessons he shared with me. That journal became my constant companion and prized possession. The lessons became more than static principles; they provided life-giving nourishment to my soul in a world of stress and responsibility and worry. The lessons became flowing grace, mountain streams to be caught up in and carried along by.

The next week I told Scotty about the lessons of grace. "What do you think?" I asked. "Can we study them and flesh them out together?"

I wanted my wife, my daughters, and the people I counseled every week to experience what I was experiencing. I wanted them to live more peaceful lives too. "My dream is for people to hear what I get to hear," I said to him.

This book exists because Scotty said yes.

●　　●　　●

We all want to navigate life with a sense of meaning and inner calm. The reality is that some days are like flowing streams, welcoming us to wade and float, while others seem to be barely a trickle, with nothing but mud to travel upon. As we move through this spectrum of days that range from dry to overflowing, it can be easy to ignore the immense interior life driving us the entire time.

That's what this book is about: your inner life.

When Scotty and I began our conversations, I desperately needed to pay attention to what was happening inside of me, or soon enough I may have broken apart. And I should note that this doesn't just happen to pastors. It happens to all of us—it's part of being human. And we all need guides along the way.

It turns out that what's going on inside of us is what fuels our decisions, activity, and peace while on this earth. What I've learned over the last decade of working with people is that the soul is often restless. As a pastor, I've had hundreds of conversations in counseling sessions, and most of them have something to do with the person, at any age or stage or situation of life, lacking peace. The details change: sometimes the catalyst is a relationship or marriage issue; other times it's a job problem or money constraints. Sometimes the person is wrestling with loneliness or anxiety, or perhaps they're struggling through something more philosophical, such as finding their meaning or purpose or value. But at the core, it's always about resisting grace while desiring peace.

When our souls are out of rhythm, life becomes a song turned to chaos. It's a reality everyone knows: we all want to be at peace, but from time to time—or perhaps most of the time—it eludes us. We want that refreshing stream, but we can't find it. Or we find a stream, but when we try to grasp it, it passes through our fingers and rushes away.

The ancient Hebrews used the word *shalom* for peace. This rich word also means wholeness, health, and blessing. This idea of shalom reflects the idea of perfect harmony with God, nature, and ourselves—something human beings have craved since the beginning of Creation. It's a completeness—an inner stillness. It's green pastures, with a stream running through, for the soul.

Shalom.

We wonder where it went, why it's so elusive, and how we can find it.

The question we all ask is, *Where can I find peace?*

Jesus said, "Peace I leave with you; my peace I give to you. Not as the world gives do I give to you. Let not your hearts be troubled, neither let them be afraid" (John 14:27). Yet even if we know in our heads that God wants us to live in peace, we don't always experience that peace as a reality in our day-to-day lives. Instead, our souls are filled with the hum of inner discontent.

But Jesus said shalom is something he gives; it's not something we work hard to accomplish on our own. And if peace is of divine origin, then we know it does, in fact, exist. Of course, we will not obtain perfect peace while in this imperfect world. But perhaps the gift being offered is a sublime song to guide our souls along the way until that day when our deepest longings for peace are fulfilled.

We all share the same struggle for peace. The stories are different, but we are all saying the same thing. We are toiling for shalom, but it's not something we can earn. It's not something we can produce. We can only receive it, sit in it, bask in it. This is what Scotty and I call living in the peace of God, and that's what this book is all about. If you find yourself longing for peace, come and join me in the loft of the barn and receive what God has for you: grace and peace.

◦   ◦   ◦

From Scotty
The Soul

It proved to be the right setting for Russ's and my relationship to begin, this barn with campfires and wooden rocking chairs. I was sharing from the book of Jonah—a portion of Scripture God had been using in my own life to reveal the disconnect between my head and my heart. Like Jonah, I had a far better theology of grace than experience of it.

After twenty-six years of being a senior pastor, I was four years into a new season of life and ministry. Having been freed from the responsibilities of senior pastor, I was given the title pastor for preaching, teaching, and worship. But the burnout from which I had never fully recovered was screaming for attention. Ministry-generated burnout is deceptive. We spin it as though we're "sacrificing for God." But in reality, with few boundaries and little accountability, vocational idolatry is a genuine threat. I was spent—emotionally, mentally, physically, and spiritually. As with Jonah, the God of all grace was beckoning me onto a healing path. There's no evidence Jonah responded to that call of grace well, and I didn't want to be that guy.

Ever since I became a Christian as a senior in high school, I'd never doubted having peace *with* God. But my inner experience of the peace *of* God ebbed and flowed between the crosscurrents of shame and grace, fear and acceptance. I was more certain about going to heaven when I died than getting healthy and free while I lived. These were some of the ideas I was musing about with the group of guys who had gathered for the retreat.

As Russ hung around me on that porch, it became obvious he didn't just want to banter theology, ministry, or sports. He had questions about my story, my heart, and some of the things I'd shared in my talks. His inner world needed attending.

Jesus summarized the Scriptures as a call to love God with all our heart, soul, strength, and mind (see Luke 10:27). In essence,

God created us to live in a vital relationship with himself—to love, worship, and enjoy him with everything we have and are. As the biblical story unfolds, we discover that we love God in response to his great love for us in Jesus. God's love for us is the meaning, motivation, and means of our love for him. The more alive we are to the love of God, the more deeply and consistently we will experience his peace.

The Hebrew culture into which Jesus was born viewed people holistically—an integrated being (soul) with multiple capacities. As image bearers of God, we are created to reflect God's beauty with our whole being. According to Scripture, God views us as whole, integrated beings—worshiping, feeling, thinking, choosing beings. In a profound sense, our soul is not something we have; it's who we are, inhabiting a body that God has graciously given us.

Because of sin and death, we live as restless strangers and foolish rebels, resisting the love of God. No wonder we experience so little lasting peace. Our thinking has been darkened. Our hearts have been seduced by a multitude of God-substitutes—what the Bible calls idols. We keep running to things that will never give us the peace we long for. We are insatiably thirsty and hungry, yet we binge on things that will never slake our thirst or satisfy our deepest hunger. It's our very desperation that makes us prime candidates for the disruptive, liberating, transforming grace of God.

THE ACCEPTANCE
WE CRAVE IS FREE.

The Restlessness Within

I WAS EIGHT YEARS OLD the first time I felt shame. My family lived in a split level in a suburb northeast of Atlanta, the last town before development turned to farmland. The neighborhood was safe, the schools were good, and droves of kids roamed the streets looking to play. It was 1980s middle-class America at its finest.

All the boys in the neighborhood were a few years older than I was. But I was all legs—a foot taller than anyone else my age—and as fast as a rabbit, so I was allowed to be part of their games. One sunny autumn day after school, we dropped our backpacks on our porches and headed to my neighbor's front yard for a football game. As always, I ran for my life, trying to avoid any contact with the older, meatier boys. I don't remember who won or what prompted the coolest boy to say these words, but after the game, he looked at me and announced in front of everyone, "You're nothing but a toothpick."

All the other boys bent over in laughter, howling and pointing out my bony knees and pointy shoulders. I fired back a few comments, the best an eight-year-old could do under the spotlight of criticism, but the damage was done. I was exposed, and for the first time in my life, I felt the hot knife of shame in my gut.

That day a change happened inside me. I became aware that I was different from the rest of the boys, and I decided that my scrawny bone structure and complete lack of mass were something I needed to cover. The way I saw it, performance was the answer. I would achieve. I would exceed expectations. I would be so good that no one would notice my deficits. My fear of being excluded created a toxic value—one I didn't grow out of the way I grew out of my Nikes. It's the poison I still drink too often: *if I'm shining enough, they won't notice what's behind the light.*

When I was in eighth grade, our school basketball team had study hall before practice. Our team piled into a classroom to finish homework and waste time talking and fooling around. Jimmy was our best player—a full-grown man at age fourteen. He dunked the basketball during every practice and every game. People drove from all over the county to watch us play, packing gyms to the rafters to see this physical phenomenon manhandle and dunk over predeveloped adolescent boys.

Sometimes in study hall, all the guys would verbally rip on each other. If you misstepped or misspoke, you became a victim. For some reason Jimmy chose to single me out one day: "You're so skinny you can't even get wet in the shower."

All of the boys fell out of their chairs laughing.

I snapped back, "Screw you, until you learn to read."

Jimmy was struggling with his grades at the time, and everyone knew it. With one blow, he could've ended my life, but he laughed me off. I wasn't worth the swing of his arm.

And it wasn't just my physical stature that pushed my shame buttons. One Friday my friend Brian came to my house to play basketball and spend the night. As we walked down the street to Ben's house to play two-on-two, I had to share a dreaded truth with Brian: my parents were getting a divorce.

We walked down the road from my house to Ben's, each of us dribbling a basketball on the hot black asphalt. I knew I needed to tell him before arriving, so as we headed out, I fumbled through the words: "Brian . . . um, I need to tell you something. My parents are getting a divorce, so my dad won't be home tonight."

My heart raced in the two seconds of silence, but Brian didn't seem to care about my startling revelation—or if he did, he didn't show it. He was a loyal friend, and he simply accepted my hurt and my new family dynamic. Although he cast no shame on me, I knew deep down that a shift had happened—inside of me, at least.

Brian had two parents at home, and so did Ben. Our small traditional town was filled with two-parent homes. Again, I felt like I needed to prove something—to show the world that I wasn't "less than." I decided I would excel at everything—grades, sports, and popularity. That would be my ticket to avoid pain and gain other people's approval.

Shine bright, young boy, I told myself.

Later that year, my grandfather began to wither from cancer, and it soon became clear that he was dying. Gramps was intelligent, well traveled, incredibly bald, and a tender, ever-supportive figure in my life. He gave me money when I made As on my report card, and he also opened an investment account in my name to teach me the power of compounding interest. He embraced me in congratulations after I scored twenty points in a basketball game, and he also snuggled up next to me on the couch after a long, ordinary day.

And then he was gone. It was my first experience with death, and as a fragile teenager, I felt like the losses were mounting, one on top of the other.

This year of loss, as I can see now, changed me at my core. Fear and shame rooted further into my soul. That's not to say I wasn't cared for. And I was never abused or neglected. I always felt loved, yet I always felt different. I harbored a deep-seated fear: *if I don't win (or win them over), I wouldn't be accepted.*

When I was in high school, my quest to perform and avoid the pain of loss only intensified. I used three-pointers, good grades, humor, even leadership in a Christian club to make sure I was known. All of this made me "somebody"—or so I believed.

As a college student at the University of Georgia, I filled my life to capacity. I was always in a hurry, always rushing on to the next thing, always working to do things faster and better. I was constantly striving to prove my worth, whether I was with my friends, working out, going on outdoor adventures, or participating in campus Bible studies. I was wading in and out of the grace of God, in and out of allowing myself to be fully loved and at rest.

From an outside perspective, it looked like I was cool, calm, and succeeding. I breezed through college, reading as many theological writings as I did textbooks on finance and marketing. After graduating with a marketing degree a semester early, I knew my next step would be to attend seminary to learn more about God.

I thought, *If only I could learn enough, maybe I could rest.*

I assumed, *If only I had a grand purpose in life, I would be satisfied.*

But on the inside, cracks were starting to form. Performing and staying busy were failing to create the peace my heart craved.

Soul-Filling Satisfaction

ONE NIGHT IN SEVENTH GRADE when I was sleeping over at Brian's house, we were playing one-on-one basketball in his driveway. But darkness overtook the goal and we could no longer see well enough to play, so we walked down the street to borrow a lantern from a neighbor. We walked up a long driveway to an A-frame house surrounded by tall Georgia pines. In the garage floodlights, a sixth-grade girl with curly red hair was practicing cheerleading jumps. Brian asked about the lantern, and we retrieved it out of the garage, said a quick goodbye, and returned to our basketball game.

Three years later I met the girl . . . Kristy.

Kristy and I grew up together. Sometimes on Friday afternoons, when she was fifteen and didn't have her license, I would drive her home from school and run my Toyota four-wheel-drive truck off the road just to hear her scream. We dated each other's friends in high school, but we never dated. After years at different colleges, she transferred to the University of Georgia as I was finishing my senior year. We rekindled our friendship, running together twice a week, talking as we covered the miles of trails around Athens. Without intention, our hearts melted together, and while I attended seminary, we began dating. We fell in love, and I married that lovely girl in June of 2004.

A month before our wedding, I graduated with my seminary degree. I naively assumed that a line of churches and organizations would be waiting to hire me after graduation, but it turned out I was the one waiting. It took two years of sending out résumés and going to interviews, with enough rejection emails to clog any inbox, before I finally received an offer as an associate pastor at a large, prestigious church in Atlanta. This wonderful church was in the wealthiest zip code in the state. It looked like a castle, with a sanctuary reminiscent of a European cathedral.

I attended the interview in the only pair of khaki pants and button-down shirt I owned. I wore my only suit for the second interview and was relieved there wasn't a third interview because I was out of clothes.

When I received the job offer, I felt like the doors of opportunity had opened before me. The first Sunday, as Kristy and I sat in the crowd of two thousand people, the pastor introduced me, and the church applauded my arrival. I was enamored. I worked my hardest to be a good pastor to these kind and smart people. I studied, wrote, edited, and preached until my hands ached from carpal tunnel and my voice required warm tea.

After eight years of learning and pastoring at this church, two families from a town twenty minutes north asked if I would be interested in starting a church. I shuddered at the thought. But I also loved the idea of creating a new place where the message of grace could be communicated without conditions or distractions. I was afraid of the possibility of failing, but Kristy and I felt called, so we ultimately took the step onto a new path to start a church and make a new beginning. In my heart, the fear of not shining never stopped.

Shine bright, young boy. Shine bright.

This drive to perform created an unhealthy pattern for my heart. There was a core tension in my soul that was growing impossible to ignore. I knew in my mind that I was radically accepted by God, without conditions. But something in my heart resisted this truth. Objectively, I knew that God could never love me more than he already does, but functionally, I often bought into the idea that I needed more than his love.

I can see now how fear was the root of my angst and anxiousness. Every Sunday I taught that God loves us without reservation, and I spoke this truth to people who came to me privately in confession and brokenness. But there was a disconnect between my head and my heart, between my words and what I actually believed.

I knew the right answers. But I didn't feel God delighting in me. As Scotty told me later, "You can know the lyric of the gospel but not hear the music."

◉　　◉　　◉

This root of fear took hold well before my birth in 1979. Ever since sin and death invaded God's world in Genesis, we have questioned God's love for us. We have doubted our welcome and our wholeness.

In the first few chapters of Genesis, the first man and woman are afraid.

Afraid of the one who never needed them but desired them and greatly delighted in them, they hid.

Afraid of each other, they blamed and shamed each other.

Afraid of themselves, they covered their nakedness with wilting fig leaves.

Shalom had been shattered, and peace had been violated.

Fear haunts and hounds my heart too.

How broken is my brokenness? I wonder. *Is there beauty still in me?*

I am afraid, so I hide.

As often as I'd been taught about (and even preached about) God's love, my heart was feeling more unsettled than content. My fears felt larger than the love. Fear of loss, fear of loneliness, fear of not being enough and not having enough, fear of exposure, fear of death—there are as many fears in the heart as there are galaxies. Those swirling fears were distracting me from God's gentle yet persistent question. It's the same question he'd asked Adam and Eve so long ago—one he asks for our benefit, not for his information:

"Where are you?"

We may be prone to wander, but he is even more prone to seek and to find.

It's a testimony to the ultimate Author that the most repeated command in the Bible isn't some form of "Get your act together" but rather, "Do not be afraid." That command shows up through-out the Bible, not as an indictment but as an invitation. I needed to learn that God meets me in my fears—the very place I run from.

We all wrestle with fear, although the specific fears—and the way we deal with those fears—vary from person to person. Scotty's story is shaped by chapters of loss and by the fear of abandonment. For him, life has been about medicating pain and avoiding more loss, while the core question that has haunted my heart is *How do I perform well enough to be accepted?* So I became funny, smart, athletic, and even religious, all in service of the question *Am I okay?* And out of this fear, a toxic value emerged: *acceptance comes by performance.*

I've always resonated with Anne Lamott's thoughts about the fleeting nature of success. In her book *Plan B*, she writes that as she moved from obscurity toward all the things that culture claims will "quiet the throbbing anxiety" inside us, she achieved "some stature, the respect of other writers, even a low-grade fame. The culture says these things will save you, as long as you also manage to keep your weight down. But the culture lies."[1]

Lamott writes about what we all must learn: the supposed paths of peace that this world promotes are no more than pieces of paper, applause that fades, and structures that rot.

    ◉   ◉   ◉

Once our new church began, Sunday afternoons became the most debilitating time of the week. In my insecurity, I questioned the success of the morning and the value of my work.

Was I convincing or inspiring?
Was I engaging enough?
Was my ego at work, or was I laboring in love?
Was my sermon good?
Was this church working?

I had to face the facts: even if everyone launching our new church was completely committed to the cause, and even if they loved me and approved of me, this would not give my soul the satisfaction I was looking for.

I recognized myself in the weary, broken woman in John 4, who finally encountered a well that would satisfy her soul's thirst. Jesus sought her out and told her of her many sins, loving her all the while. "Jesus said to her, 'Everyone who drinks of this water will be thirsty again, but whoever drinks of the water that I will give him will never be thirsty again. The water that I will give him will become in him a spring of water welling up to eternal life'" (John 4:13-14). The well of performance and approval left me feeling continually parched. I needed a well that would truly slake my thirst.

As the renowned nineteenth-century preacher Charles Spurgeon said, "Your life consists not in what you possess, nor in what you lack. You shall find in Christ a fullness, a soul-filling satisfaction."[2]

I longed for this "soul-filling satisfaction," but I still wasn't sure if I *truly* believed I could be fully known and fully loved. And even if I did believe, when and where and how would I begin to feel it?

●   ●   ●

From Scotty
I Was Eleven

It was October of 1961. I sped home as fast as my feet could pedal my bike the two miles between Graham Elementary and 532 Oakwood Lane. I was ready to fish, and Johnson's Pond was a mere five hundred yards from my house. As I rounded the corner, slicing through the crisp autumn air, our home came into view.

I couldn't wait to see Mom. She lit up every space she inhabited, and her welcome was my first hint of the goodness of God.

But immediately I noticed Mom's car wasn't in our driveway, which struck me as a bit odd. After owning and managing a children's clothing store (Scotty's Children's Shop) in Greensboro, she had left the business world to enjoy her dream home, which my parents had built three years earlier. She was always home when I came barreling in after school.

I looked for a note on the table but found nothing. I figured she must have run out on an errand. Knowing time was ticking before I needed to report back for Dad's prescribed suppertime, I grabbed my fishing rod and some pieces of raw bacon for bait and bolted out the door.

Fishing was a safe, happy place for me as a kid—a refuge, an adventure, a dream factory. I was content to fish alone . . . except on the days I caught a whopper. Those are the days a fisherman wants to hoist his catch and say to a friend (or even a stranger), "Hey, check this out!" This would be one of those days.

Under a Carolina-blue sky, I cast my line toward one of my favorite spots, close to the cattails. Johnson's Pond was filled with hungry bream and some really nice bass. My bobber disappeared faster than I could set my hook. Fortunately, the beast on the other end of my line swallowed my hook and weight, and nearly the entire bobber too. I tried to stay calm, figuring it might be a big bass. I fought him onto shore—it was the biggest catfish I'd ever seen. I looked to the right and the left, wanting to show my trophy fish to someone. I'd never seen a catfish in Johnson's Pond. For that matter, I'd never seen a monster like this *anywhere*.

Having swallowed my hook, the fish died quickly, so I decided to take him home to show Mom. I put him on a makeshift stringer and proudly started the quarter-mile walk home. In sight of our house, I could see that Mom's car still wasn't in the driveway.

Then I saw Mrs. Peters, our neighbor from across the street, walking toward me. She didn't look at my catfish. She looked as if she'd seen a ghost.

"Scotty, I'm so sorry . . ."

Beauty from the Beginning

I PULLED UP TO THE BRICK TWO STORY and began to gather the mess of items in the passenger seat that had collected over the four-hour drive to Franklin, Tennessee—fast-food wrappers, water bottles, my rambling thoughts scribbled on a notepad. My heart was pounding a few beats faster, excited for the day, as Scotty walked outside. As his little dog ran off to do her business, we walked inside, and he showed me around, pointing out the place in the sunroom where he sits when we talk.

We were now a year into our friendship, and by this point we'd logged hundreds of hours talking, texting, and video chatting. We were modern pen pals, so I recognized most of the home, having already seen it through the lens of his iPad. We finally settled into a living room above the garage. The room was large, with bookshelves and cabinets lining the walls. The space was filled with books, pictures of his family and friends, and keepsakes from trips. An exercise bike sat in the corner, and a bank of windows let in warm light.

Scotty sat facing me in a wooden armchair, his legs crossed and his bare toes sticking out from his Birkenstocks.

"Mom died instantly in a head-on car crash in 1961," he said, startling me with how quickly he began his story of loss. "My dad, my brother, and I lost the single person who was the joy, laughter, and life in our family. We were emotionally gutted that day. Dad was a good man, but he worked harder at providing for us than being there for my brother and me."

"What was that like?" I asked.

"With Mom gone, our home screamed the absence of beauty, affirmation, and love. Dad shut down emotionally. He grew distant and quite depressed. I have no memory of his touching me, in either affection or discipline. There were no hellos when I entered the home and no goodbyes when I left."

There was a moment of quiet between us, and I tried to picture the layers of loss this story represented for Scotty.

"In that environment of disconnect, I learned to live like an orphan in my own home," he went on. "Hiding became my modus operandi. I thought, *If I can just keep from upsetting Dad, everything will be okay.* I learned to be present while staying distant, compliant without being connected. This carried over into all my relationships, including my marriage."

Scotty told his story effortlessly, like a song that had been rehearsed for decades. He shared the details without shame, yet with genuine sadness. His honesty and openness never stopped surprising me. Most of us are wary of revealing our brokenness because we wonder if someone could love us if they knew our imperfections.

"You turned to hiding. I turn to performing," I said. "My story is: I'll perform at basketball. And when that ends, I figure, okay, this religion thing's working out. I'll perform at being good and insightful. The pastor thing—this is getting some praise. Let me get onstage and earn some applause."

"You perform, and I hide, but it's really the same thing," Scotty said. "It's just a different strategy. We avoid our shame, fear, and pain while at the same time ignoring our beauty and worth. We say to our world, 'Come close, but not too close. Notice me, but don't know me.'"

●   ●   ●

Later that week, as I reflected on Scotty's words, I was reminded of the first poem of the Bible and how it speaks to our beauty and worth. "In the beginning, God created the heavens and the earth" (Genesis 1:1). This God is a creating God—the Hebrew name used in this verse is *Elohim*, denoting supremacy.

In the second verse, we see that the Spirit of God is hovering over a wild and formless world, like a loving mother warming her unborn creation. At that point God speaks the Creation into being and begins to name things as *good*. The day and night, the oceans and stars, and the flying and running and climbing creatures. They—and all of Creation—are *good*.

Then, as the grand finale for his entire Creation, God said, "Let us make mankind in our image" (Genesis 1:26, NIV). And while he deems everything else good, he declares people *very good*.

What does it mean for God to call us—to call *me*—"very good"?

C. S. Lewis gets to the heart of that matter in *The Weight of*

Glory: "There are no *ordinary* people. You have never talked to a mere mortal. Nations, cultures, arts, civilisations—these are mortal, and their life is to ours as the life of a gnat. But it is immortals whom we joke with, work with, marry, snub, and exploit."[3] God was pursuing me with this truth: I hold dignity and worth, beauty beyond beauty, because God spoke it as true from the beginning.

While studying Genesis, I discovered the word *perichoresis*, a Greek word meaning "rotation." In the fourth century, some Christian leaders began to use the word to describe the Trinity: God the Father, God the Son (Jesus), and God the Spirit (the Holy Spirit). Perichoresis is the image of a dance. Franciscan priest and author Richard Rohr calls the Trinity "the circle dance of love."[4]

I have participated in a perichoresis of sorts in my own home. In the evenings after dinner and bath time and before our three little girls are tucked in for the night, our little family has dance parties in our den. We play music and form a circle, and we all dance freely and unabashedly, without hesitation. Inside that dance of love, posing and pretense has no place.

When I feel the pressure to perform, to deliver, to succeed, these moments of dancing in the den offer me a taste of the Trinity, helping me to grow in my awareness of the immeasurable delight God holds for me. My salvation lies in knowing this great love, and my joy is found in reminding myself time and again that in Christ Jesus, I don't need to prove my worth.

I am already accepted.

I'm already in the dance.

The Acceptance Given

IT'S EASY TO BELIEVE the false promises of drivenness: do more, be more, accumulate more . . . and then you can be happy. I often fall for the trick, believing that the next (and bigger) house or car or achievement will solve my inner problems.

During one conversation when we were talking about acceptance, I told Scotty, "My dream is to sit in the back of a large room where everybody in the room—thousands of people—know who I am but don't know I'm there. They're all impressed by some achievement I've made, but I'm not required to talk to anyone. I have performed, and people know me and respect me, but I don't have to be known."

"It's hard to believe that God made us for intimacy with himself and others, not primarily for our usefulness to him, isn't it?" Scotty responded. "Most of our relationships are hardwired for performance-based acceptability. That means by nature, we are allergic to grace. We've grown up in a world of scorecards, thermometers, charts, and trophies. We work hard to win, but so often we lose at love."

"That's probably true for me," I said. "I want to be accepted, but I don't really want to be known."

We all fall into the temptation of substituting something else for real acceptance. Look pretty. Make the grade. Get the job. Be better. Write a book. Do well. Get a sculpted body. Make more money. Get the house. Own the mountain cabin. Shop more. Find romance. But underneath those accomplishments are deeper needs, deeper questions.

Am I okay?
Am I beautiful?
Am I enough?
Am I _____?

As soon as I answer the question "Am I okay?" with anything other than the promise and provision of my belovedness in Christ, I drift toward anxiety and darkness. Yes, there is a temporary high from the offerings of the world, but after the high fades, the sense of lostness and wandering returns.

As Scotty put it, "Apart from the garments of God's grace—given to us freely in the gospel—we'll reach for the rags of some futile covering. Shame has to do with being seen, and we are convinced that being fully seen by God would destroy us. To be seen as we really are is just too much to fathom. Our guilt and shame demand a payment we can't pay." Scotty was saying that as long as I live as a stranger to the love of God, I will try to outrun or silence my own shame. But avoiding my shame doesn't get rid of the shame; instead, it fertilizes it. Before long shame sprouts poisoned fruit that ranges from impatience and anger to covetousness and lust. I try to cover my wounds, but a Band-Aid is no help for a cancer. Shame's unrelenting declaration is:

You aren't enough.
You aren't welcome.
You aren't loved.

○   ○   ○

I remember watching Jean Paul Gaultier, the renowned French fashion designer, interview Lady Gaga, the music megastar. They talked about her life, career, and philosophy. Gaga projected a message of radical acceptance. Be yourself, she encouraged her fans. Be a "little monster." Yet toward the end of the interview, she said something fascinating.

> I think it's why I like fashion and style so much. I feel the ability to create an alternate fantasy and reality for myself that, if I do it over and over again every single day of my life, falling asleep in my wigs, my makeup, my jewelry, my dresses, then somehow my fantasy becomes my reality.[5]

As Gaga finished the interview, I wondered, *Do I really have to keep wearing my wigs?* Is this the way to accept my little monster self? Do I have to live in fantasy to cope with reality, to find peace?

Six years after the interview with Gaultier, Gaga filmed another documentary, *Gaga: Five Foot Two*. While her style and creativity remained, something had changed:

> I never felt comfortable enough to sing and just be
> this way now, to just sing or wear my hair back. I never
> felt pretty enough or smart enough or a good enough
> musician. That's the good part—the good part is that I
> just didn't feel good enough and I do now. . . . I know I'm
> worth something. So I just have to stay there.[6]

When shame is driving my quest for acceptance, it's not enough to fashion wigs for my little monster self. I'm learning what Gaga has seemingly learned: that it's impossible to find self-acceptance if we continually cover up who we are. It leaves us always dressing up but never at peace as our true selves. Peace arrives only when we stare down the little monster and see that we are not just different; we are actually broken.

That's the bad news. But there's good news too: we are accepted by our Creator precisely in that cracked condition. We are known and loved, and therefore secure beyond our abilities and accomplishments. We're worthy simply because we're beloved.

Author and priest Henri Nouwen writes, "Over the years, I have come to realize that the greatest trap in our life is not success, popularity, or power, but self-rejection. . . . Self-rejection is the greatest enemy of the spiritual life because it contradicts the sacred voice that calls us the 'Beloved.' Being the Beloved expresses the core truth of our existence."[7]

The acceptance we long for is not self-acceptance, or even others-acceptance; it's divine acceptance—a welcome and delight freely given to us by the one who created us. Only God's grace can dispel the darkness in my soul. It's frightening, really: the way light shines into my darkness is through the cracks of my broken self. But if I'm willing to take that risk, I can be welcomed and exist in the holy beam as God's forever beloved.

In the Genesis story, when Adam and Eve came out from their hiding place, they stood clothed in those flimsy rags they'd made from leaves. God asked them, "Who told you that you were naked?" (Genesis 3:11) as if to ask, "What happened?" It was their chance for honesty, not shame. God was simply trying to get them to come clean. His voice was the voice of love.

The good news about grace is that in our fickleness—as we strive, hide, blame, and sometimes even repent, the voice of God keeps calling to us. "What happened?" God asks. In other words:

Are you ready to be seen?
Are you ready to talk?

•   •   •

From Scotty
I Was Fourteen

It was September of 1964. I walked down the hall of Graham High School, making my way to the freshman lockers with a couple of buddies by my side. All the normal fears and insecurities of being a ninth grader coursed through my body. But they were lame compared to the greater fears, anxieties, and pain that lay dormant in my heart. Dormant . . . but about to be awakened.

Just before I rounded the corner, in front of the collected treasures of the GHS athletic department, I saw our head football coach coming toward me. I knew him, not because I was on the team, but because we both lived on Oakwood Lane, and I mowed his grass in the summer. I thought, *Okay, this will be cool. Coach will greet me, and some of my friends will be impressed that he knows me on a first-name basis. This could be good.*

Three feet in front of me, Coach B. stopped. I expected to see his arm extend for a handshake and then hear my name called: "Welcome, Scotty. Finding your way around okay?" But Coach didn't extend his hand. He might as well have been wielding a chainsaw. He looked me over from my head all the way down to my feet and then, making sure he made eye contact with me, said, "I'd be so ashamed if I had a body like yours."

And then he walked off.

It would have been harmful enough if Coach B. had called me to his office to offer commentary on my pudgy frame, but to publicly shame me in front of my friends was abusive. I was humiliated, objectified, and dehumanized. I immediately became that ninth-grade boy who was vexed whenever the bell rang for PE class because I had to undress in front of my peers. The curse of comparison entered my life.

Like a searing brand that burned a new identity into my soul, Coach B.'s comment marked me with a new name: fat, out-of-shape kid. But it was more than a name; it redefined how I viewed myself—a poisonous, indelible tattoo. I tried to pass it off, minimize the trauma, and humor my way out of the shame, but none of it worked. Something changed deep inside me that day. I became shame's prisoner—first through the loss of my mom and now through the loss of my dignity.

Of all the enemies of peace, shame is at the top. The names on our birth certificates are written with mere ink; the names written on our hearts by evil and by failure—and by some people we should be able to trust—have been inscribed with permanent marker. Only the grace of God can possibly begin to rewrite our shame.

I experienced release from my guilt decades before I entered the healing journey of God's grace for my shame. Partly because I confused the two. And partly because of fear. But even as the Spirit has led me from one story of my brokenness to another, so Jesus has been faithful to give me grace upon grace.

Belovedness as Identity

Scotty told me that between his freshman and sophomore year of high school, he furiously tried to sabotage his shame. He determined to never let anyone speak to his heart in such a demeaning way again. So began his obsession with losing weight.

During the summer of 1965, he consumed little more than heads of lettuce and, as a nonrunner, ran scores of miles in the heat. He lost forty pounds while growing six inches. He left the comfort of food for the power of control—first over his weight and then over a whole slew of things. The quest to be noticed but not known became Scotty's strategy for relating to just about everyone.

Listening to Scotty share this out loud made me wonder, *Is my hunt for acceptance the reason I feel restless?*

Idols don't remain idle. Until I rest in the abiding peace that only comes from knowing my identity in Christ, I stay on the hunt for my next deliverer, finding that one after another is a pretender. I give too much power to these false offers of peace: the approval of others, the desire to be noticed but not known. Idols place impossible demands on me and drive me further from God and his grace.

This self-propulsion from one idol to the next, without contemplation or confession, is sin. Sin insists that I forget my dependence on God and rely solely on myself. What Martin Luther described is true: sin is the heart "curved in on itself."[8]

Sin and shame both tell me a false story about myself and God:

You aren't enough.
You aren't as beautiful as she is.
You aren't as successful as he is.
You need a little more of that.
You need a little less of that.
God doesn't really care.
God will care . . . if you will only _____ .

Sin creates shame, and shame arouses further sin and despair. The two work together, keeping us on paths of control, performance, and hiding. Some people recoil at the notion of sin because it implies judgment. But denying the truth of sin while seeking self-knowledge is like losing your car keys in your house. You frantically search every room. You look on shelves and tables first, then under blankets and cushions. Your frustration builds as your search continues because you need those keys to get to where you're going. A day goes by, and then a week, and finally you turn your head and there they are, sitting on your nightstand.

They were there the entire time, but you weren't aware of it. And that lack of awareness was the very thing causing your frustration. The concept of sin is right in front of us—actually *in* us. In me.

In a *New York Times* op-ed, Crispin Sartwell, a professor of philosophy at Dickinson College, wrote an article entitled "What's So Good about Original Sin?" In this piece he argues that even if we forget the Bible's assertions, there's a secular argument for original sin.

> When I look within, I see certain extreme failings. I have not been able to get rid of most of them, and I have accumulated others as I've gone along. Perhaps you've done better, but most of us certainly come up short of our own ideals, ones I hope most people, religious or not, generally share—to be generous, peaceful, energetic in helping others and hesitant to help ourselves at their expense; to take care of the world we inhabit; to not only not kill one another (or even think about it), but to love one another. Even by our own mortal standards, we are profoundly flawed.[9]

Even the most apparently put together among us don't have a full handle on life and faith—or even ourselves. It's impossible for me to read the Bible with any honesty and not feel crushed by it in time: *Be holy. Pray always. Rejoice in all things. Don't be anxious. Don't hold on to anger. Never lust.* In Mark 12, Jesus says the greatest commandment is to love God and our neighbor with an agape (unselfish and unconditional) love. These callings guide me but then break me, not because the calling is lacking in holiness, but rather because I am lacking in perfection. This reminds me of what Paul says: "All have sinned and fall short of the glory of God" (Romans 3:23).

The reason I feel imperfect (even as a person of faith) is because I *am* imperfect. Not without beauty or worth, but always with imperfection. Broken. My heart is marred and marked, if not by deed, then certainly by motive. To accept "I am imperfect" is to see my diagnosis clearly, even as I see a God who forgives me and loves me as I am, while also setting me free to become more than I am.

●   ●   ●

When I was working at the large church in Atlanta, I knew God regarded me one way—in grace—but I lived another way—by means of an exhausting life of self-assessment, devoid of grace. I constantly gauged how I was doing by keeping an internal scorecard. And the wearying thing about my scorecard is that I never scored enough.[10]

Every evening as I drove the twenty-five minutes on the expressway from the church to our little craftsman house, I pondered how good this faith was if I was feeling imprisoned by it. I wasn't going to walk away from Christianity, but I was beginning to see why people do.

In this season of moralistic imprisonment, due entirely to my making a faith of freedom into a faith of merit, I discovered two verses and clung to them for dear life: "As far as the east is from the west, so far does he remove our transgressions from us" (Psalm 103:12) and "For our sake [God] made [Jesus] to be sin who knew no sin, so that in him we might *become* the righteousness of God" (2 Corinthians 5:21, emphasis added).[11]

This convergence of forgiveness and righteousness *by gift alone* rescued me.

I was at the end of my rope not because the gospel was false but because I wasn't resting in the entirety of its goodness. The truth that I was forgiven *and* fully righteous, by no work of my own, created a seismic shift in my soul. This revelation brought me from religious merit to gospel relief. If I am already forever forgiven and forever made pure and righteous by God, then it's impossible for God to have a scorecard where he tallies and ranks my every action. And my internal scorecard could be transformed into greater rest in God's delight in me.

This truth felt like a fresh mountain stream after drudging through a desert. It was love, not fear. It's always love or fear, and as we were leaving the safe haven of our large established church for an unstable start-up, I would need more than ever the promises of love to become my resting place.

From Scotty
Prayerful Contemplation

1. As a child, where did you feel most known and loved, desired and safe? Who gave you your first taste of welcome and acceptance?

2. When did acceptance begin to move from a given reality to an earned one? In other words, when do you first remember feeling like you didn't measure up—that you weren't doing enough or being enough?

3. What were your earliest thoughts about God? Was he someone to trust or avoid? How has your understanding about God's acceptance of you changed over the years?

4. Where do you tend to turn when God's acceptance doesn't seem to be enough to fill your deep longing for acceptance and peace?

5. Who introduced you to the radical mercy and grace of God?

6. Where are you currently in your journey of coming alive to God's lavish love for you in Jesus?

THE SECOND CONVERSATION

SURRENDER, NOT CONTROL, IS THE PATH TO PEACE.

God's Forever Love

"I THINK I'M HEALTHIEST when I'm disconnected from my work," I said to Scotty. He and Kristy and I were eating dinner together at a local restaurant in our town. It was his first visit to see us, and I was excited for Kristy to meet him and for all of us to be together.

"What do you mean, 'disconnected'?" he asked.

"I mean I feel healthiest emotionally when there's a distance between my heart and my work."

Neither of them appeared to agree with me, and I wondered if I was speaking too swiftly on an empty stomach, halfway through a cocktail.

"Maybe *disconnected* is the wrong word," I backtracked. "It sounds unloving to my work."

"Yes, it's the wrong word," Scotty said sympathetically. "You don't need disconnection. Better to think in terms of a reorientation with your work, a healthy engagement with your calling and with the one who has called you to himself. The problem isn't with work per se; it's with the power you've given your work to give you peace—or to rob you of it."

At the time, still early on in our church, our little start-up was drawing people who were eager to learn and generous in spirit. Small groups and Bible studies with spiritually engaged leaders were being formed. The metaphorical pews weren't empty, yet I could still feel that my inner peace was overly dependent upon the pews being full.

As I walked away from the table that night, I thought about how easy it is to hitch ourselves to the wrong peace wagon. If we assume that our deepest fulfillment and satisfaction can be found in work, romance, kids, possessions, or anything else other than the love of God, we'll put expectations on those things that they can't deliver. And we'll never find the peace God made us to experience.

To live in the peace of God, we have to know that God is not a threat and that nothing can threaten his love for us.

⊙   ⊙   ⊙

"The Bible doesn't call for a surrender to a God who is a distant dad or power-hungry authoritarian figure," Scotty told me, "but to a gentle, loving Papa."

This was not a new idea for me, but it did send me into a renewed contemplation on the image of fatherhood in the Bible. Most of the references to God as a Father are in the New Testament. The term *pater*, Greek for "father," is the most common term Jesus used to speak about and address God. And there is an even more intimate term that Jesus and Paul both used for God: Abba.

The word *Abba*—most closely translated "Papa" in English—was not used by servants or slaves but was reserved only for beloved children. When Jesus and Paul called on Abba, they were proclaiming the father-child bond between God and his people. The first-century Jewish culture they were speaking to held massive respect for and awe of God. They didn't even speak God's name aloud, and when they wrote it, they left out the vowels as a symbol of reverence. Jesus revolutionized their understanding of faith. He maintained the holiness of God while simultaneously proclaiming the love the Father holds for us and the intimacy he desires with us.

Abba is the name Jesus used for God in Mark 14:36 when he prayed in the garden of Gethsemane, just before being arrested and taken to the Cross. In his despair, Jesus was longing for protection, care, and love from his Father.

Abba speaks of tender endearment and trust by a child toward a father. The Father loves me tenderly, and he is bound to me like a father to his child. With an attachment so tangible, undeniable, and unbreakable, I am free to come close to him, to know him, and to have him know me.

In my family, my daughters tend to have full days of school, gymnastics, and playing outside. Kristy and I end the day snuggling each of our daughters into their beds, asking what's going on in their hearts and praying for them. Despite my imperfection as an earthly father, they snuggle in close. They soak in a sense of security and connection.

When I understand God as a tender Papa who welcomes me ever near, my heart opens to him in return. God doesn't want to zap me; he longs to welcome me as his child, just as I do with my girls.

Brennan Manning, the brilliant writer of *Abba's Child*, wrote, "Define yourself radically as one beloved by God. This is the true self. Every other identity is illusion."[1]

Our understanding of God as Abba changes everything, including our very identity. Our Father doesn't fix us so that we no longer have any problems. He welcomes us to come to him with our problems, knowing we'll be met with love.

Why would we choose to operate as orphans, resisting the love that heals us?

How could we forget our identity as children of a Papa who will never stop loving us?

The Insufficiency of Control

THE AGONY SHOT INTO MY CHEST as I tried to stand up from the leather armchair in my living room. I made it halfway to standing before the pain increased, and I froze. After a moment, I pressed my feet into the rug and rose another inch but had to stop again. I stabilized myself with the sides of the chair and slowly sat down again, waiting for the pain to fade. The whispers of shame began inside my head.

I'm a failure. I can't hold it together.
I can't manage my life, and I'm having a heart attack before the age of forty.

"I can't stand up," I called to Kristy, who was in the kitchen. "My chest . . . it fills with pain when I stand up. It really hurts." I massaged my heart with my right hand.

"Okay, okay, slow your breathing down." She sat down next to me. "Do we need to go to the hospital?"

"No, just let me rest a bit. Let's see if it goes away."

Two days later I drove toward Atlanta for an appointment with my primary care physician. From the outside, it seemed like everything in my life was going well. Our church was launched and in its first year of bonding and growing. I couldn't have asked for a more loving and nonjudgmental group of people to work with and build a community with. I had a charming town to raise my daughters in. And my wife was supporting me through all this with her trademark affection and force. Yet there I was, driving south toward the city to have my heart checked.

I shouldn't feel upended or anxious, I thought. *I have a good life.*

"How are you feeling?" my doctor asked.

"I'm here." I laughed nervously. "I think my heart is failing. There's an intense pain in my chest and the side of my neck and in between my shoulder blades in my back."

"Okay, well, what's going on in your life right now?" she asked.

I told her about our lovely town and our amazing church community and my great wife and darling daughters. I also told her I felt like there was a house of cards I was managing, and it might crumble at any moment.

"So you have stress," she said kindly. "I see this a lot, Russ. You are probably stressed."

I'd never thought of myself as a stressed person, even though the symptoms were all there: low energy, headaches, worry, apathy, five too many episodes of *The Office* late into the night. The doctor pressed circular, multicolored stickers across my chest, and thin wires ran from the stickers to a machine beside the bed. The test began, beeping every once in a while, and all I could think was, *How did I get here?* and *How does this get better?*

"Your heart is fine," she said. "You didn't have a heart attack. You're having heart palpitations caused by stress, so you need to take it easy."

"What does *easy* mean?" I asked.

"It means you have to find things that help you manage your stress. Places that slow you down."

Manage my stress? Slow down? I scoffed internally. *Can I move to Maui? Maybe more wine would work?* But of course, even if I moved to an island or drowned my anxiety, whatever I was avoiding and whatever I was covering up would still be there. I am wherever I go, and the problem is inside me.

I wasn't quite sure how to explain this to the doctor, but sometimes it felt like there was a stubborn little man in my chest who was continually clenching his fists. How could I tell him he was no longer welcome?

Priest and author Henri Nouwen wrote this profound prayer:

Dear God,
I am so afraid to open my clenched fists!
Who will I be when I have nothing left to hold on to?
Who will I be when I stand before you with empty hands?
Please help me to gradually open my hands
and to discover that I am not what I own,
but what you want to give me.
And what you want to give me is love—
unconditional, everlasting love.
Amen.[2]

●　　●　　●

One of my favorite movies is *The Shawshank Redemption*. I've spent countless Saturday afternoons watching this movie in bits and pieces as I flip between it and a football game. There's a key scene when the prisoners are sitting on the bleachers in the prison yard. Their friend Brooks has been released after fifty years of imprisonment. Brooks is free, yet he doesn't know how to operate in that freedom. All the boundaries and structures of control that ordered his life in prison are gone. Without the walls there, he doesn't know what to do in this new world and he becomes anxious and afraid. He thinks about committing a crime so he can return to prison, and eventually he kills himself.

Morgan Freeman's character, Red, explains the way prison seeps into a prisoner's being:

> In here, he's an important man, he's an educated man. Outside he's nothin'—just a used-up con with arthritis in both hands. Probably couldn't get a library card if he tried. . . . These walls are funny. First you hate 'em, then you get used to 'em. Enough time passes, it gets so you depend on 'em.[3]

I think this disbelief and discomfort with freedom is why many of us swing from religious control to control of another kind: rebellion, doubt, or burnout. Or we swing in the opposite direction: from rebellion to overzealous piety and self-righteousness. Either way, we are attempting to exert control, refusing the free acceptance, forgiveness, and righteousness Christ gives.

Of course we have to control certain aspects of our lives: we have to keep the car between the lines on the road to avoid a wreck or work hard to learn a new skill or show up to work to get paid. Control helps us exist in the world without constantly destroying each other, but inevitably we overdo it. Rather than embracing the freedom and grace we have in Christ, we attempt to use control to find validation and acceptance.

> *If I can only control that coworker, then I will be . . .*
> *If I can only control that child, then I will be . . .*
> *If I can only control this sickness, then I will be . . .*
> *If I can only control this traffic, then I will be . . .*
> *If I can only control this timetable, this project, or this perception of me, then I will be . . .*

But this formula never works. Inevitably, even if we achieve the thing we're trying to control, another "something" to control replaces the first something. All the while, control limits the very life it promises as it produces an unending demand for us to perform. I'm learning that control is the opposite of faith. It's the power grab that originated in the Creation story, when those two chose to eat the fruit in an attempt to hold power that's intended for God alone.

As I struggle with the powerlessness I sense inside myself, I try to reach for power that's beyond my limitations. This creates more exhaustion and condemnation in my heart. Eventually control chips away at my relationships, building walls around my heart.

◉   ◉   ◉

Last week I looked out the front window of our house and watched my six-year-old skipping down the sidewalk. She was by herself, moving from a group of friends in one yard to another group of friends in another yard. That night as I tucked her into bed, I asked her what she loved about playing outside.

"I feel free," she said.

My daughter's unencumbered, unapologetic joy reminds me of the childlike faith Jesus calls me to. It's no wonder she feels free. When she's playing outside, she has no chore list to complete, no schoolwork to turn in. The record keeping has stopped. She can simply be her true self. Of course, there are still expectations. Consequences still exist. But the pressure is gone, and in that freedom, her soul is at rest and playfulness abounds.

My skipping daughter knows the freedom I desire and need.

Per my doctor's orders, I began taking more walks through the tall pines and broad oaks of Kennesaw national park near our home. I asked God for a greater awareness of the tight places in my heart. I prayed that he would help me release the things I was clinging to so tightly for control. It didn't happen overnight, but week by week, walk by walk, I felt myself start to unclench. The stress began to come in visiting storms rather than in a constantly hovering hurricane.

I couldn't see where all this was headed, but God was beginning a work of peace in me. So two months after my doctor's visit, when I was sitting in the loft of that barn, with my doctor visit fresh in my mind, I was ready for what Scotty had to say. I was prepared to hear someone talk without restraint about his wins and his wounds, and about a kind of freedom that carries us beyond the insufficiency of control and into the streams of grace.

● ● ●

From Scotty
I Was Seventeen

It was March of 1968. Forty pounds lighter and a foot taller than when I'd gone by the nickname "Meatball," I began to live wild as a senior in high school. My insecurities and heart wounds were held at bay by the "coolness" of playing in a band and the consumption of just enough alcohol. My older brother, Moose, and I grew up immersed in beach music—not the West Coast surfer music of the Beach Boys, but the shag-dancing music of Motown. Moose was a gifted musician, and his band used to back up groups like the Temptations and the Four Tops.

Moose taught me how to play the keyboard, and he got me a job playing organ in a local band called the Originals. I spent most weekends of my senior year traveling to university campuses between Washington, DC, and Athens, Georgia, to provide the dancing and drinking music for fraternity parties. I was seventeen years old, making good money, and living a party on wheels. With no curfew or parental intervention, I was the envy of my classmates.

Fortunately, God began to disrupt my life when my friend Steve became a Christian. Nearly 100 percent of my peers attended some kind of church—it's just what you did living south of the Mason-Dixon Line in the sixties. I always assumed I was a Christian, attending church with my dad and brother about as much as any of my peers.

Steve loved me enough to invite me to see a film created by the Billy Graham Evangelistic Association called *The Restless Ones*. At the time I had a cute girlfriend, money in my pocket, and another weekend gig coming up. Those things consumed most of my thoughts, and I held little expectation sitting there in the State Theatre in downtown Burlington, North Carolina.

The movie itself was nothing to rave about, but at the end of the movie, when Billy Graham came on the screen, I was riveted by every word he said. It felt like he was speaking directly to me about the kindness and power of a God who was pursuing me.

An invitation was given to trust Jesus—to accept the free gift of eternal life. I responded by walking to the front of the theater, where I was welcomed and prayed for by one of the trained Billy Graham Association counselors. Immediately, I felt a lightness, a peace, and a "rightness" of heart I'd never experienced before. I didn't see dancing angels or visions of heaven, and I didn't make any promises to become a missionary. All I knew was that everything had just changed—in me and for me.

My slate was clean; I had a new start. It was not a bad beginning into faith, but I held a woefully inadequate understanding of what really happened when I became a Christian. My fear of guilt and death were gone, but it would be many years before I could say the same thing about my fear of shame and life.

The Effect of Weariness

A FEW YEARS INTO LAUNCHING OUR CHURCH, things were going according to plan. Our governing board of directors was united, and our monthly meetings were filled with prayer, planning, and laughter. We had a staff of four and had bought a warehouse to renovate into a church building. The shabby was becoming shinier—or at least less shabby—but the inner parts of me were still fragile, waiting for the house of cards to crumble.

I kept telling myself there was an altitude, a view ahead, that would calm all the restless parts of my soul. In my low moments, I would buy a Lotto ticket with a hot dog at the gas station and envision ridiculous scenarios of being flooded with money and opening a quaint retreat center in the San Juan Mountains of Colorado.

One morning, when I was feeling particularly discouraged, I sent a text to Scotty. "When you feel like you want to quit and walk away, is that true? Is it burnout, or is it 'seasonal disinterest'?"

I waited for an answer, for those magical lights on my phone to blink. I needed something to settle me.

"Russ, a normal life, like the beach you love so much, ebbs and flows," he replied. "A healthy person embraces both the highs and lows of life. The key is to live in the tension with perspective and wisdom. Only take responsibility for what you can control, and don't be controlled by the people and things God hasn't given you control over."

"So, more surrender?" I asked.

"Yes, but not surrender like shrugging your shoulders or begrudgingly giving in. We're talking about the surrender of your heart to your good and loving Father."

"Am I so tired because I'm resting in the wrong thing?" I asked. "Is that why I want to run?"

"Exactly," he wrote. "You *are* tired. The gospel doesn't make us superhuman but more fully human. God doesn't love us as we should be but as we actually are in any given season. Take time to marinate in the goodness of the gospel, and fill your heart with God's love for you in Jesus."

There was a pause, and then my phone flashed again. "He doesn't just love you; he enjoys you. He delights in you as his child."

I took it in, letting Scotty's words ground me, even though everything in me wanted to run.

"Have you ever thought about quitting?" I typed. I deleted the words once and then retyped them. Was I being too bold to ask Scotty about his weaknesses? I swallowed hard and pressed send.

"Absolutely, many times!" he replied. "Maybe I'd become a chef, a fly-fishing guide, or a photographer. Anything but a pastor."

I breathed a sigh of relief and kept reading. "When we feel

like running from something—whether it's a job, a spouse, or some perceived threat, we need to slow down. Core emotions like anger, fear, and anxiety are voices of the heart, and we need to figure out what's really going on in our hearts. There really could be a five-alarm fire. Or we might just need a nap. In fact, sometimes the most godly thing we can do is take a nap."

"Thank you. You're right," I wrote. "I'll be better tomorrow."

Of course, I wouldn't magically be better tomorrow. But I was beginning to realize that the faster I could catch myself drowning, the faster I could turn to Abba and ask for help.

Our Identity as the Beloved

I LIKED THE THOUGHT OF WALKING AWAY more than the reality of it. I only talked to Scotty and Kristy about those feelings. Who else could I tell? I was trying to convince people to be a part of our church and then, during the week, convince myself to stay. It was helpful to hear from Scotty that I was probably just tired. In a way, I was overcomplicating it all—questioning my calling and my position in life rather than simply admitting I was weary in mind, heart, and body.

I don't think I'm alone in these feelings of soul weariness.

We're constantly looking for life, but we don't want to give up our illusion of control. We want resurrection to new life without a crucifying death. A friend of mine says that wherever you are weary, the "law" is at work. And so we get even more tired and perhaps cause destruction—or by the grace of God, fire off a text about quitting a thing we love.

The apostle Paul wrote about the law in his letter to the Galatians, who had lost sight of the freedom they once knew. They had learned of their forever acceptance by God in Christ and then returned to merit to feel loved and valued. The law is the right standard of God for us. It's all of the holy and good shoulds of Scripture. Here's what Paul writes about the law and faith:

> O foolish Galatians! Who has bewitched you? It was before your eyes that Jesus Christ was publicly portrayed as crucified. Let me ask you only this: Did you receive the Spirit *by works of the law or by hearing with faith*? Are you so foolish? Having begun by the Spirit, are you now being perfected by the flesh?
>
> GALATIANS 3:1-3, EMPHASIS ADDED

Like the Galatians, I heard the gospel, happily receiving the love of God and surrendering to Christ, but then I made faith about what I did for him (and what I did in the world). So of course my box-checking, performance-obsessed, praise-seeking way of life was creating greater and greater exhaustion in my heart. The law was holy, but I was incapable before it, crushed under it as imperfect. I had to let the law crush me so it could guide me to the life of accepting that I was enough by grace alone, through faith alone.

It's easy to convert from the many forms of irreligion in our culture to a form of religion and never convert to the way of grace in Christ. As my understanding of the role law played became clearer, my imprisonment to it also became clearer. I was left at the end of myself and wondering, *Where do I get relief?*

I was looking for the right life, the perfect life, the perfect escape. But what I was really looking for was the perfect love.

Scotty often reminds me this is why Adam and Eve made their own fig-leaf clothing. We can't ignore our fears of being exposed, failing, and "sucking" at life. Neither can we deny our God-given longings to matter and have impact in the world. Our natural inclination is to form our own covering (justifying ourselves through the law and our own efforts), yet God enters the Garden and calls us out from our hiding. And this gracious God doesn't condemn us but loves us. He replaces our inadequate coverings with a more substantial covering—by sacrificing not just an animal, as he did for Adam and Eve, but his own Son. At a great cost to himself, God grants us welcome and reconciliation. In a very real sense, we receive his forgiveness as a garment of grace. Scotty put it like this: "Any religion based on rule keeping sabotages the notion of a loving relationship. I believe this is the primary perversion of the gospel."

⊙　　⊙　　⊙

One episode of the podcast *This American Life* features an interview with chef Dan Barber.[4] The interview is about foie gras, or goose liver. The method to produce this delicacy is horrific, as animals are bound and force-fed through long tubes for weeks until their livers are overgrown.

But there's a farmer in Spain named Eduardo Sousa who has a different strategy. He has a flock of geese that are free, without cages or fences, and yet the geese never leave him. His geese reproduce constantly, and their livers are as plump as the finest chefs in the world would desire.

When the podcast hosts arrived to interview Sousa, they found him lying in the grass alongside his geese, saying over and over again, "Lovelies, lovelies, lovelies, come around, lovelies. Over here, lovelies."

Sousa said, "You don't have to force-feed geese to get them to gorge out on food, because geese gorge themselves naturally in the wild." So Sousa has his geese on a farm without roof, walls, or fence.

Free as a bird, you might say.

The geese wander and fly, but they always return because the food is abundant, and the love is lavish. The key, according to Sousa, is that the geese have to know they are free before they feed.

There's a story in Scripture that says essentially the same thing. Only in this case, the farmer is God and the one flying free is Abraham. In Genesis 15, God said to Abraham, "I will bless you."

Abraham's response was, basically, "How do I know? How can I be sure?"

I would have a few questions myself. *Bless me how? Based on what? Can I really fly free?*

God replied, "Well, here's what I want you to do. I want you to kill some animals and cut the animals into pieces and arrange the pieces in two rows, with an aisle."

Now, this request seems odd to us, but this was the normal practice by which covenants (binding commitments) were made between two parties. If a person of great stature desired to make a covenant with a lowly peasant or servant, animals were killed and ripped in two. The servant took an oath of loyalty to the great man by walking between the pieces and saying something like, "I swear loyalty to you, oh lord. And if I do not keep my promise, may I be cut into pieces like this."

So Abraham assumed he was arranging for a covenant ceremony. He killed the animals and cut the pieces. But when darkness came, a fiery pillar passed between the pieces. God walked through, and Abraham never had to. God was saying, "I will bless you when you obey, and I will also bless you when you don't obey." As pastor and author Tim Keller teaches, God is the one who upholds this relationship, not us.[5]

God is not hovering over us, watching for every slipup, and ranking us. He's not saying, "Okay, I did my part; now you do yours. I got you in the dance—now you'd better dance perfectly to stay at the party." The commitment God made to Abraham, and by extension to us, is made in love, sealed and worked out by God alone.

If faith is nothing more than our commitment to God, then we are thrust into a constant state of anxiety as we measure and gauge that commitment.

How true was the commitment I made?
How strong was my commitment?
Is my commitment as strong and passionate as it used to be?

Scotty said to me, "As Christians, we often have the idea that our assurance and peace depend on how strong our faith is. But we are not in relationship with God only to the extent that we are *like* Christ. We are in relationship to God to the degree that we are *in* Christ, which is 100 percent. When Jesus said it was enough to have faith the size of a mustard seed, he was saying, 'Take measurement out of the equation.'"

Faith isn't measuring up to some impossible standard; it's the ability to hear the forever whisper in and over us, *Lovelies, lovelies, lovelies, come around, lovelies. Over here, lovelies.*

Collapsing on Jesus

SCOTTY MENTIONED IT IN PASSING ONE DAY—a casual reference to taking a nap—but I remembered. I always remember a napper, especially a midweek napper, which is the most committed form. Scotty takes a nap almost every day for twenty or twenty-five minutes, "a splendid subterranean grace practice," he calls it.

It would be easy to excuse the nap as the normal practice of a seventy-year-old man, but Scotty has never seemed seventy to me. He rises early in the morning, before the sun, to study the Scriptures and pray—"communing with God," he calls it. After his personal time with God, he writes prayers and sends them out to tens of thousands of people online. His days are filled with teaching interns at his church and spending time with pastors to guide their inner lives toward grace and growth. Some days he has lunch with his wife or works out at the community center. He likes to ride his bike along the river near his house. He has just as many opportunities to speak and write as he did ten or twenty years ago, but most days, by midafternoon, you will find him in complete nothingness—the grace that comes on the other side of drivenness.

My wife, Kristy, comes from a long line of nappers. When she was growing up, her family could be found cozied up and conked out on couches on Saturday and Sunday afternoons. At my house, in contrast, weekends were filled with yard work and tennis. It took ten years of marriage before I began to give in to this mid-day practice of surrender. I'm a slow learner, I suppose. But now, every once in a while (even midweek!), just to be a rebel against the world, I lie on the bed next to my writing desk in our bonus room and close my eyes.

Theologian Frederick Buechner offers this perspective on sleep in his book *Whistling in the Dark*:

> It's a surrender, a laying down of arms. Whatever plans you're making, whatever work you're up to your ears in, whatever pleasures you're enjoying, whatever sorrows or anxieties or problems you're in the midst of, you set them aside, find a place to stretch out somewhere, close your eyes, and wait for sleep.[6]

Buechner says that sleep is the definitive reminder that all the things we think make us the people we think we are must, in fact, stop. At least once a day, all our earning and relentless striving stops. The heart still beats and the lungs still function, yet we are wonderfully unaware, surrendered, and finally not attempting to govern our lives.

In surrendering to God, as in the surrender of sleep, we concede that we rest in him—outside our own efforts, capabilities, or merit. This surrender, this resting in him, is also the essence of repentance. In the kindness of God, repentance is not the fear that he will strike us but the falling into a love greater than any other love.

Scotty's spiritual father was a pastor and seminary professor named Jack Miller. Scotty quotes Jack all the time, casually beginning every tenth sentence or so with the phrase, "My spiritual father, Jack Miller, said . . ." Well, Jack Miller said that repentance is "our ongoing calling to collapse on Jesus, acknowledging our need and receiving his supply."

In Luke 15, the younger son disrespectfully asks for and takes his portion of the inheritance from his father and wanders off to a foreign country. He parties and wastes money, seeking temporary pleasure, escapist dreams, and the approval of people. It works for a while, but in time the money runs out and the friends leave. He's left working a farm, poor and hungry, longing for the food the pigs eat. He sees the nothingness of his life. But there is a sliver of hope left in his mind, one likely placed there by years of kindness from his father.

The son thinks, *If I return home, perhaps my father will take me in.*

So the prodigal begins home and practices his plea of repentance and surrender on the journey. As he nears home, his father sees him from a distance and runs to him. The son begins his repentant speech, not knowing if the father will reject him or embrace him. When his father reaches him, he wraps his arms around him and kisses him. The father throws a robe around his boy and begins to plan a party in his son's honor.

The focus shifts from the son to the father's love. This is the arc of the Bible: every story builds to a human understanding of a heavenly Abba who loves and embraces us.

When we stop insisting, like obstinate children, that we can do it ourselves; when we stop fighting and lower our shields, we find divine embrace. When we collapse from the exhaustion of resisting the loving Father, we can quit trying to earn back his love with pious pretense and enjoy the freedom he offers. It's then that we rest.

⊙　　⊙　　⊙

From Scotty
I Was Eighteen

It was September of 1968, six months after awakening to Christ's sufficient forgiveness and love for me. I was a freshman at the University of North Carolina at Chapel Hill. It was the sixties, and revolution was in the air.

"Down with authority" was the message.

"All we need is love" was the culture.

It was a struggle for me to attend class. I was sleeping in after late nights at nearby concert halls, singing and dancing to the likes of Tina Turner, Joe Cocker, and Grand Funk. I was immersed in two very different worlds: the music of the times and the Bible.

The first Bible study I attended on campus was filled with believers whose Bibles showed wear and tear, with favorite passages marked. My Bible stood out, shiny and untouched, so I skipped several days of class to read through the entire New Testament, frantically underlining anything that seemed to be a key verse, alternating between three colored pens. I told myself I was doing it at this crazed speed out of fullness of heart to know God.

I can see now that I was projecting onto God the only experience of *father* I was familiar with—a man who wasn't physically or emotionally engaged with my life but had high expectations of me. I began to think of God as a more benevolent version of my dad. I wasn't afraid of angering God, as I was Dad. But I felt I needed to do something each day to please him, which in reality was more like appeasing him. Spiritual disciplines such as reading the Bible and memorizing verses became less a means of grace to me and more a way to self-righteousness.

Although this kind of thinking is often normative in Christian subculture, it's actually antigospel. Implicitly and explicitly, we are taught that "doing it right" will bring blessings while reducing suffering in life. Read the Bible more, memorize verses, pray longer, witness to more people, and obey the rules, and God will love you more—and reward you with good stuff.

"We get what we deserve; we get what we earn." That theology marked the way I functioned in life. But that is the way of karma, not the way of grace.

Wholeness Is a Gift

I WAS THIRTEEN YEARS OLD—a hurting boy, as I can see now—lying in my bed, with a massive Michael Jordan poster hanging on the wall over my head. I was trying to fall asleep when I heard from the core of my being, *You can know me as a Father*. It was a spiritual hearing of some sort, not an auditory voice in the room. I know some would say this message was self-created, but I believe it was God. It was as real as the bed I was lying in and the air I was breathing.

I've never walked an aisle or prayed a prayer to pinpoint a specific "moment of salvation," but I know Love, and I have no doubt the voice of Love was calling me that night. As much as a thirteen-year-old could, I sensed a pursuing, divine compassion, more profound than anything this world could offer. My spiritual senses came alive to the world's brokenness, my sin, and God's encompassing love.

But although I knew of my sin at the age of thirteen—and even twenty years into my faith—I didn't understand my shame or its repercussions. I knew about the promise of heaven, but I didn't understand the promise of wholeness.

◎   ◎   ◎

As Scotty shared more of his story with me, he kept alluding to a scene from *The Wizard of Oz*. "Like Oz, I was living behind the curtain," he'd say. Or "By God's grace, I finally came out from behind the curtain."

I'd seen the movie as a boy, but I'd never read the original book by L. Frank Baum written in 1900. I knew the story outline: Dorothy is stranded in the strange, fantastical land of Oz, wishing to return to her home in Kansas. This quest leads her down the yellow brick road toward Emerald City, where she'd meet the Wizard of Oz, who would supposedly help her get home. On the way, she meets the Scarecrow, the Tin Man, and the Cowardly Lion, all of whom have their own fears and desires.

"I was the Wizard, standing behind curtains, pushing ministry buttons, emitting the illusion of competence," Scotty said. "I had a very utilitarian self-image. I was more comfortable being useful to the Lord from behind the scenes than entering my brokenness and joining the Tin Man, the Scarecrow, Dorothy, and the Cowardly Lion in the journey of getting healthy and finding home."

My conversations with Scotty were revealing to me that even if I was pushing very helpful buttons, like preaching and teaching, I didn't need to hide behind curtains. I needed to come out and be with everybody else, to *own* my brokenness and enter God's story of healing and transformation.

Oz came out from behind the curtain when Toto entered. I think of my exhaustion and anxiety as the "Toto" God sent to bring me out from behind the curtain of my own making. The providence of exposure almost always comes with some measure of pain. But it isn't meant to humiliate us; it's intended to humble us. It isn't meant to shame us but to free us.

I knew I needed to come out of hiding, but I wasn't quite sure where to start. So I bought a copy of *The Wizard of Oz* and sat on my front porch and read. I didn't read the book to analyze it; I read it hoping it would analyze me, to see if it would reveal that I, too, am the man behind the curtain.

Oz doesn't appear in the story until the end of the book, and while reading the pages to get there, I found myself in each of the characters along the way.

Like Dorothy, I seek a sense of home and peace.

Like the Scarecrow, I want to be smart and think rightly about life and this world.

Like the Tin Man, I desire to care and love.

Like the Cowardly Lion, I want to be courageous.

I then found each of these characters reflected in Oz. He becomes the mirror revealing not only the characters in the story but all of us who are hiding behind our carefully drawn curtains. At some level, we are all afraid that the way we think or love or struggle or persevere—the way we are—isn't enough to deserve acceptance. So we figure it's safer to stay behind the curtain.

This book isn't intended to be a spiritual allegory, but I found God on its pages—not in Oz or his pretense as the Wizard, but hidden in the love of Dorothy for her three hurting friends. This love is seen as she tells the Scarecrow, just as he is leaving to receive his brain, "I have always liked you as you were."[7] While the Scarecrow, the Tin Man, and the Cowardly Lion struggle with feelings of inadequacy throughout the story, Dorothy and the reader see glimpses of the very things they seek—brain, heart, and courage. In reality, they aren't wrestling with perceived deficiencies; they are wrestling with how they might be accepted and loved.

It turns out that wholeness isn't about magically getting that thing we lack; it's about surrendering to the God who already accepts us and graciously absolves us of sin. It's only then that we can come out from behind the curtain without fear and in peace.

But it's difficult to surrender to a way of grace when it contradicts the way we grew up. My socialization through education, sports, and activities created a deep-rooted value system that claimed, "You get what you deserve" or "You are what you earn."

Even while in churches, I was shaped by my performance-based assumptions that manifested in distorted theology and toxic, angst-filled living. So while grace may be taught from the pulpit, it doesn't always take root. We might talk about it on Sunday, but we struggle to believe it and rest in it on Monday.

"Why do you think that doing more and trying harder is going to put a bigger smile on God's face?" Scotty asked me one day. "He already loves you as much as he loves Jesus. There's nothing you can do about it but believe it, rest in it, and serve him *from*, not *for*, his delight. Quit 'should-ing' all over yourself."

God isn't comparing me to someone else or keeping score. He's not assaulting me with condemning questions:

Why aren't you like your sister?
Why can't you get your act together?
Why did you screw that up?
Why aren't you more motivated?

If we are in Christ, we never lack his love; we only lack resting in it. We don't need to pretend anymore. We can walk out from behind the curtain of a performance-driven life. There's no doubt this is an act of surrender—it's a risk to step out to be loved by our Abba. But when we do, we can experience his lavish love—even if we're not the smartest, most loving, or bravest child around.

From Scotty
Prayerful Contemplation

1. How do you see the conflict between surrender and control playing out in your life? What do you work hard to control? Which parts of your life are the hardest to surrender to your Abba Father?

2. Whether you recognize it or not, the Holy Spirit is constantly telling your heart that you are God's beloved child. What voices do you tend to hear louder and believe more than the Spirit's reminder of your belovedness?

3. What lies, false promises, or illusions have you hitched your "peace wagon" to? Finish these sentences:

   "I will only have peace when . . ."
   "The biggest obstacle to my inner peace is . . ."

4. Where do you usually take your fears, shame, guilt, and longings? Who typically pays the price for your inability or unwillingness to rest in the love and grace of God?

5. In God's kindness, you are given affirmation and a new identity. He says, "You are mine" and "I love you as you are." In him, you matter, you belong, you are enough, and you are forgiven. What would change in your life if you truly embraced that new identity as God's beloved?

RECEIVING, NOT ACHIEVING, TAMES OUR FEARS AND ANXIETIES.

If You Build It . . .

"Morning, Scotty," I texted. "Please pray for me. I'm very anxious. I'm spending too much time in my head, and I'm losing peaceful moments."

This particular anxiety was the result of decreasing cash flow at our church. It was nothing catastrophic, but it was concerning enough that our leadership was monitoring it. If the decrease became normative, we would have to make sacrifices, and the two other full-time employees and I would feel it.

Scotty knew what was going on at the church, and he replied almost immediately. "Will pray. Let's see what God does. Share how you're feeling with Kristy, and ask if she's noticed this anxiety showing itself in you. Make sure you ask her to pray for you."

"Okay," I said. "Thanks."

●　　●　　●

Six months after Scotty visited us, I returned to Nashville to see him.

He met me in the driveway. "Let's talk at the church. The little dog is just too yippy," he said, sliding into my car.

"My car is a mess," I said. "Sorry." I began tossing empty water bottles and a shoebox from the floorboard to the backseat. Scotty had on his normal attire—hiking pants, a casual plaid button-down with a T-shirt underneath, and his worn-in Birkenstocks. He always looks more like a whitewater-rafting guide than a pastor.

The church Scotty started is a massive brick block of a building on a wide stretch of land along a highway in Franklin, Tennessee, just outside of Nashville. The building has a contemporary angled entrance that shoots out into the parking lot, and the main lobby is several stories tall, with light pouring in from above.

As I stood in the entryway, I tried to imagine the amount of work it took to design and construct such a place. And the practical work came after the more abstract—and important—task: gathering people, leading them, and bonding them together as a gracious church with an enduring vision.

I thought about our little church, already five years into existence. It was growing, but it was nothing like this, not close to this scale. I told myself I didn't need big numbers or a beautiful building to be fulfilled, and most of the time I believed it. But there was also the insecure part of me that believed otherwise.

When I think about building something, I recall the famous quote from the movie *Field of Dreams*: "If you build it, they will come." I've always loved that movie—partly because I love to create new things. I like the idea of something tangible coming from nothing. The movie has always inspired me to be a person who steps into challenges, even when it seems impossible.

But when I watched the movie again several years ago, I found myself a wreck on the couch, tears streaming down my face. I didn't know why at first. Perhaps the loving family in the movie got to me, or maybe it was the lonely writer who found meaning again, or maybe it was the reconciliation between a father and his son. At any rate, the music broke something loose in me, and my heart longed for the kind of shalom the characters experienced under the field lights. I wanted to be in a place like that—free of pressure, performance, and pretending.

Of course, we don't live in a field of dreams, and our lives don't wrap up as neatly as a two-hour Hollywood film. The only way for us to encounter this kind of freedom is to take in the heavenly Father's gift of acceptance. When we receive the truth of our belovedness, we receive the nourishing, never-ending grace that brings life to the inner self.

In the Old Testament, King David received this revelation of love. He caught sight of his brokenness after being confronted about his affair with Bathsheba. He had been arrogant in taking Bathsheba for himself, disloyal in his attempt to cover up his sin, and callous in arranging the murder of Bathsheba's innocent husband, who was David's loyal friend and soldier.

When he was confronted by the prophet Nathan, David confessed his sin and surrendered. Later in life, he wrote about the love he continued to experience as he let go of his grip on control and took in the constant goodness of our God: "The LORD is gracious and merciful, slow to anger and abounding in steadfast love. The LORD is good to all, and his mercy is over all that he has made" (Psalm 145:8-9).

Even when my feelings tell me otherwise, God is not angry with me.

He takes my sin seriously, but the price of that sin was paid for on the Cross.

He pursues me with love, whether I'm resisting him or resting in him.

It's the most freeing thing of all, this life in the peace of God. The question isn't whether the welcome and love is present for me; the question is if I'm ready to give up the performing and pretending so I can live in the grace and peace that is offered.

◎   ◎   ◎

From Scotty
I Was Thirty-Four

It was January of 1984. Along with three friends, I'd signed up for a pastoral-counseling intensive with Dan Allender at Grace Seminary in Winona Lake, Indiana, where he and Larry Crabb were teaching. I was pastor for adult discipleship and interim preaching pastor at Christ Presbyterian Church in Nashville. Darlene and I had been married twelve years; our daughter, Kristin, was eight, and our son, Scott, was five.

The format of the intensive was for us to observe Dan through a one-way mirror as he worked with a client. The counselee received free counseling in exchange for having four strangers watch, and we received the benefit of increased pastoral education.

"Hey guys, I've got some bad news and some good news," Dan told us shortly before the session. "The woman who committed a month ago to being counseled just backed out. The good news is that one of you gets some free counseling while the other three watch me work. Any volunteers?"

In a split second, without thinking, I raised my voice and my hand. "I'd love to be your guinea pig."

Just as quickly, one of my friends shouted, "Scotty, what are you thinking? You're going down, my friend." His words were prophetic, but it would take about sixteen years for his prophecy to be fulfilled.

The fact that I didn't hesitate to take Dan up on his offer says more about my denial than my courage. Dan and I had met nine years earlier when we were attending Westminster Seminary, but our relationship only became a friendship after we graduated. We reconnected when Dan began teaching with Larry Crabb and they came to Nashville to lead a seminar.

For the next four days, Dan pursued my story and my heart while my friends watched. He kept prodding, asking questions about my family, my relationship with God, and my experiences of loss and pain. I was hiding in plain sight.

"So, Scotty, it's been a while since we've been together," Dan said. "Get me caught up. How are you and Darlene doing? Anything in particular you'd like us to chat about?"

"Everything's great, Dan. Nashville rocks. The church is growing. The kids are great. As you know, Darlene is doing some important work on her story of sexual abuse. I'm very proud of her."

My rapid-fire litany of affirmations didn't impress Dan—or deceive him.

"What does it feel like to sit with Darlene in her pain? You're right, she's going to some really dark places in her story. How are her tears and her anger impacting you?"

Boom! Dan knew that's precisely what I *wasn't* doing. I was an incarnation of Carly Simon's song from the sixties "Haven't Got Time for the Pain." I confused transparency with vulnerability. I owned the data of my story but avoided the heart-shaping implications of my trauma. I thought I was being strong by muscling through the loss of my mother and pressing into my role as a busy pastor and father. What I didn't realize was that my denial wasn't just suffocating my own growth; it was also snuffing out my ability to empathize with the pain of others. If we don't make time for our own stories of loss, pain, and grief, we certainly won't make time for anybody else's sadness and heartache.

I never felt threatened or vulnerable as I talked to Dan—just intrigued, even mystified, as I experienced his skill as a therapist. That's a confession, not a boast. Indeed, Dan was, and is, really good at what he does, but I was clueless about my own blind spots . . . and really committed to self-protection.

The last day, Dan summarized his observations: "Scotty, here's what stands out to me after our time together. There are two things that define you more than the love of God. First of all, you haven't begun to understand and grieve the way your mom's death impacted you. Second, you can't and won't sit still. You keep interrupting me and trying to finish my sentences. You have a noisy, restless heart. You're a runner. What do you think that's about?"

Inner Wealth

BEING A LEADER FEELS LIKE STANDING on the shore of the ocean. At times I look out to the horizon, my feet in the water, and nothing pulls on me or makes me stumble. Life is good. Then a slightly larger wave barrels in, and it forces me to step to the right or left. And at times, a riptide arrives out of nowhere and threatens to pull me under.

This isn't unique to leaders—I think most people feel this way. The waves have an undercurrent that can pull against our heels, and before we know it, anxiety has replaced our inner calm. That's when we begin to question life, comparing our circumstances to those around us.

Maybe I'm not cut out for this, we wonder.
Maybe I'm not capable.

In the first few years of shepherding our church, I thought this periodic wave that knocked me off-balance was circumstantial—something I was navigating poorly or something that required more attention than I was giving. I was convinced my anxiety was stemming from adverse situations, and if I could just change the circumstances, I'd be able to find peace. But the truth is, the circumstances only had the power to create anxiety because I was allowing my heart to rely on my work for affirmation. I bought into the false comfort that if things were going well, I was important. I mattered. I was loved.

As a result, when the waves broke, my emotions broke with them.

At the moment, our church's financial situation was the wave threatening to pull me under. We had purchased an old textile warehouse and were renovating the building so it could serve as a functioning church space. We'd also just hired a third full-time staff member. Just as these expenses were mounting, our gifts and tithing decreased.

Our decision to move forward with the building and the staff person had been made based on two years of cash flow data, so the decrease seemed like only a blip on the radar at first. But after four months, there was no change, and my stress was starting to surge. After six months, our leadership team was on high alert. I am sad to admit that in our leadership meetings, we discussed scenarios more than we prayed. As a pastor, I would have given lip service to the power of prayer. But when it came to the circumstances of my own life (and church), I was trying to maneuver my way into a healthy budget.

"We are still $4,000 a month short," I told Scotty after one leadership team meeting.

"Okay, well that's not the end of the world, based on your budget and savings," he said. "Y'all are still financially stable."

"I know. I'm just really stressed about it," I said. "I use money to feel safe, so I'm spiraling."

"What about running short stresses you the most?"

"It just makes me feel unstable, like we were when we started the church," I said. "I also remember when I was little and my parents divorced, and I watched my family go from having enough to money being tight. I've worked really hard to try not to be there again."

"I understand. Russ, we live and lead out of our wounds," Scotty replied. "Our idolatry shows up at the intersection of our woundedness and our sin. We all love control more than faith. This is just part of your growth in grace, while you learn to lead through it."

I formed a contingent budget that I brought to our next leadership meeting in October. We approved the cuts, which would begin in January. They would reduce my salary and require employees to partially pay into their health insurance. I met with our staff to share the news and pray. I resigned myself that this was the new normal and that nothing would change.

But Scotty kept saying, "Let's pray about it. Let your church know what's going on. And let's see what happens."

On a Tuesday in the beginning of December, our treasurer and another church leader called me and said they'd like to meet with me that afternoon. They walked into my office, sat down, and handed me a letter.

The elders of Christ the Redeemer Church are extremely grateful and humbled by the generosity of the donation pledged by an anonymous donor. This overwhelmingly generous gift is a testimony to Christ's active involvement in the lives of his people. And it is a tremendous encouragement to us to continue sharing the gracious gospel message of Christ. The payoff amount of Redeemer's building mortgage is $1,009,842.35 until December 15 of this year. Our understanding is that a donation of $1,007,000 will be made on or before December 15. The elders of Christ the Redeemer Church resolve that the entire donation amount will be applied toward the principal balance of the mortgage. The mortgage balance remaining will be paid by the church so as to retire the entire mortgage debt.

I read the letter a second time. The stress I'd been living with the previous six months transformed into a deep sense of gratitude. My anxiety was tamed as much by the extravagant act of grace and generosity as by the sheer monetary amount itself.

The next Sunday the leadership team gathered, and I read the letter aloud. The seven of us cried together and decided not to tell anyone until the gift arrived. Two Sundays later, I stood in front of the church and told our people that there are no small gifts and that all gifts create cash flow for ministry. There's nothing healthier than a large group of people giving. And then, every once in a while, something out of the ordinary occurs. I read the letter.

People sat stunned. People cheered. People cried.

It meant we were saving $7,350 a month, and we were free of

our mortgage debt. We owned our building and were immediately cash flow positive.

To this day, I don't know who gave the money, and I don't know why we'd be the recipients of such lavish grace. Our church thinks of that miraculous gift as part of God's story of faithfulness to us and an encouragement to our calling. All we can do with a gift like that is receive it with gratitude and be faithful stewards of what we've been given.

After church I climbed in my truck and texted Scotty. I hadn't told anyone outside our leadership team—not even him. "It's my joy to let you know an anonymous gift of $1,007,000 was given to our church, and we paid off our mortgage of $1,009,842.35," I texted him, smiling the entire time.

"Wahoooooo!" he replied. "I'm so happy for you and your church."

A GIF of Tyler Perry as Madea saying, "Hallelujer" followed.

Then there was Will Ferrell dancing and screaming, "Awesome!" after that.

●　　●　　●

It's easy for me to live with the beloved self on one proverbial shoulder and the sinful self on the other. The beloved reminds me of my identity, my forgiveness, and my righteousness in Christ: *you have a wealth in you beyond measure*, I hear. It's a wealth beyond both the circumstance of difficulty and the circumstance of abundance. The sinful false self, in contrast, whispers lies on repeat:

You need that, and then you'll be enough.

You need everything to be under control, and then you'll be enough.
You need that big gift, that big raise, and then you'll be enough.
You need that relationship, and then you'll be enough.
You need that promotion, and then you'll be enough.
You need that recognition, that person's approval, and then you'll be enough.

A few questions from Scotty have helped me see which stance I'm living in:

1. Am I living in self-dependency? Worry? Fear?
2. Am I able to accept and love others—even those who are different from me?
3. Do I feel anxious about where I stand with God?
4. Do I feel anxious day to day?
5. Do I live in apathy toward God?
6. Does my sense of security depend on my performance or on whether I attain a particular goal or desire?

When I ask myself these questions, I remember a phrase Scotty uses in sermons after he raises convicting questions: "Don't hear me saying, 'Shame on you,' but 'Grace on you and grace for you.'" In other words, he's raising the questions not to condemn but as a means of disruptive grace.

Grace will always disrupt us before it delights us.

In a short parable in Matthew, Jesus uses the image of treasure to teach us about the only wealth that is able to satisfy our impoverished and searching souls: the Kingdom of God.

> The Kingdom of Heaven is like a treasure that a man
> discovered hidden in a field. In his excitement, he hid it
> again and sold everything he owned to get enough money
> to buy the field.
>
> MATTHEW 13:44, NLT

Here comes this ordinary guy in the parable—not wealthy, not poor, just completely ordinary, as far as we know, and he's looking at some land. He walks around the land and stumbles on the treasure of a lifetime. Perhaps it's a jar of gold or silver, coins, or jewels—something magnificent. He looks around, heart pounding, to see if anyone is looking, for he knows he has no right to this treasure.

I've found this, but how do I make it mine?

In ancient times, money was a medium of exchange but not something that was saved and deposited in a bank. People didn't invest in the stock market or buy bonds. If they had wealth, they hid it for safekeeping, which made it possible for treasure to be left behind.[1] So the only way to rightfully take possession of such a treasure was to become the legal owner of the field. The lesson is not one of morality and whether the new owner was hoodwinking the previous owner but rather that there's a treasure worth so much that a person would be compelled, in joy, to let go of everything else in life just to have that one treasure.

"Everybody has a category of wealth," Scotty told me. "Every culture says, '*This* is to be desired.' So we go for that until we are awakened to 'No, *this* is worth more.' But inner wealth is a transcendent currency, something that things of external value can't increase."

The man in the parable who sold everything had nothing at the time of possession of the treasure. In essence, he lost everything to gain the treasure.

The same is true for us.

As magnificent as a huge check might be, no one can write a check large enough to compare to a heart enamored with the infinite currency of grace.

○ ○ ○

From Scotty
I Was Forty

It was February of 1990. I hate surprises, and Darlene knows it. But for my fortieth birthday, she pulled off a huge surprise that God used to begin thawing out my frozen heart.

I sat blindfolded in the passenger seat of our car, assuming we'd meet a few "safe" couples at Choices, one of my favorite restaurants in downtown Franklin. I expected warm hugs from Scott and Linda Roley, Mike and Sue Card, a nice meal, a few laughs, maybe a kind card or two. But the drive was taking a lot longer than anticipated. Just as my control monster was about to rear its ugly head, the car stopped.

Darlene took me by the hand and walked me about twenty yards. We went through a door into an eerily quiet room.

"Okay, honey, you can take off the blindfold now," she said.

As I lifted my red bandanna, I was greeted by a loud shout: "Surprise!"

Fifty well-chosen friends from different seasons and places

of my life stood smiling and cheering. As music began to fill the room, I got over the shock, calming down my inner introvert and getting myself into party mode.

My brother, Moose, now a professional musician, had put together a band to play songs from the soundtrack of our lives—the Motown-style beach music we'd played in high school and college.

Everything was great until they lit forty candles on my birthday cake and started singing. Fifty people tried to make eye contact with me, and I felt simultaneous joy and embarrassment—and maybe a bit of shame. I was so touched that these people cared enough for me to show up on a Saturday night but also really afraid of being under their scrutiny. What would they think if they truly knew me?

How long does it take to sing "Happy Birthday"? I thought the song would never end, so much so that I started singing the song along with everybody else. "Happy . . . birth . . . day . . . to . . . Scotty . . ."

My mind was racing. These were good friends, but did they really know me? Did they *really* want to be there?

Turning forty wasn't a big deal to me, but birthdays have always been an odd part of my story. I don't remember having a birthday party as a child—perhaps I've just forgotten. But I do know that after Mom died, Dad never made a fuss about February 1. In fact, after I left home, he never once called to wish me a happy birthday.

When it came down to it, I wasn't sure I was worth all this fuss. I would have rather stayed in hiding. But God, in his grace, refused to let me stay there. He pursues us to free us, and he exposes us to envelop us in his healing love.

Questions for God

I WAS TWENTY-ONE YEARS OLD, on a break after completing college in December and looking toward entering seminary the following fall. I sat on a train barreling southwest out of London into Hampshire. Station after station passed; towns and countryside blurred in the window. I dared not fall asleep, lest I end up at the coast in Portsmouth.

At last I arrived in the village of Greatham, deboarded the train, and walked the two miles to L'Abri, the manor estate turned retreat center where I would be staying for the next ten days. People come to L'Abri from all around the world to work and study, meet with theologians, and have conversations with other students.

I had a thousand questions about God and for God—questions about my life, and specifically what I might do with my life. I was also trying to make sense of traumas I'd experienced and witnessed: how living through my parents' divorce affected me; why, a few years earlier, I'd stood in the hospital with a group of people praying for two of my friends to live after they drove a speeding car into a tree; why my friends lived, only to have one of them kill herself a year later.

When I'd prayed in the aftermath of those losses, I felt like I received rejections instead of answers. And now, on the cusp of adulthood, I sensed a general gnawing uncertainty about my future. I wondered about God's will and whether prayer helped all that much in this world.

I settled into my bunk and became acquainted with a few of the guys I'd be sharing a room with: a college graduate in his midtwenties who had studied religion and art at Brown, a seminary professor from India who was taking a sabbatical to rest and study, and a student from South Korea who had stopped by for a few days in the midst of his travel.

In my first session with one of the theologians on staff, I asked, "What is God's will?"

"That subject fills volumes of books, Russ." He looked at me, waiting for me to refine my question.

"I guess I'm wondering what I'm going to do with my life. But at the same time, I'm wondering why certain stuff does or doesn't happen. How much of a say do we have in things?"

"I'll point you to some lectures to listen to and some books to read," the theologian replied. "They'll help, but all the knowledge you can gather won't bring peace if you're looking for complete certainty. We usually want a concrete lens to view God's will with, but God's will is too expansive for our viewing. It's outside time and human knowledge, so we become subject to it, subject to him. It returns us to relationship."

"What kind of relationship is that?" I asked.

"It's active passivism," he said.

Noticing the confused look on my face, he continued. "Passive activism, the other way around, means your beginning point is active. You take control. Surrender is a part of your life, but it's more words than heart. You try to control your world and other people via your actions, merit, words, and even prayer. Active passivism is the opposite posture. It begins in humble relationship with God, and you live in the universe knowing you aren't in control of suffering. You aren't in control of fixing everything. You aren't in control of causing every door to open and shut."

As he spoke, the words rang true somewhere deep inside me. As much as I wanted a predictable formula, it also felt like I was being given the key to get out of a jail cell I didn't even realize I was in.

"Your beginning point is passive, but in the passive posture, you are active," he went on. "You aren't a doormat. You speak and act and pray. This is the way of humility and peace. You are alive and active but not in control. You're trying your best while checking in regularly—that is, building a trusting relationship—with the one who is in control."

◉   ◉   ◉

It's been almost twenty years since that conversation, but I can remember it almost word for word. This was the first time I became aware of the tension between what I am able to know and what must be faith. This revelation helped settle my heart about trying to understand God's will for my future. I had been trying to solve that as if it were a math problem, but that's not how it works. I needed to allow the discovery of God's will to be relational in nature. God was welcoming me into his mystery, and my job was to say yes to his invitation.

My prayers had always been dominated by my lists for God. My focus was trying to get God to do what I wanted—or at least what I deemed best. Active passivism was not my strong suit, perhaps because it's about surrender, which runs contrary to my controlling nature.

I've prayed for people who have won their battle with cancer and lived many more years, and I've prayed for people who died of cancer at age five. I've lost three friends to suicide, all of whom were loved by God and loved God. They didn't lack faith, but their prayers weren't answered the way they desired. God heals, and God doesn't heal. God opens, and God shuts. I'm not sure how my prayer affects God. But I do believe prayer is powerful, so I continue to pray.

I appreciate the way the psalmists prayed through a range of emotions. They lived through pain and turmoil, chaos and calm—just like we do. They sang in praise, raged in anger, and wailed in lament to God. They didn't view their circumstances as reasons to avoid voicing their thoughts and emotions in prayer; instead, they earnestly spoke them to God. The Psalms grant us permission to talk to God, even in our selfishness, even in our pride, even in our doubt. We can pray, sing, and vent to God, and we can trust that God's love and power will have a transformative effect on us as we pray.

Throughout Scripture, we are told to pray—for other people,

for unity and joy, for friends and partners, and in gratitude for all of it. We hear intoxicating stories of people being prayed for and healed, but if those miracles are all we expect from prayer, we discount the power of prayer and minimize what God is accomplishing through both our comfort and our sufferings—namely, a stronger relationship with him. I continue to pray for miracles in the material world, but the bigger miracle of prayer seems to be the way prayer draws me to God.

I've spent my life surrounded by people of prayer. Over time I've concluded there are two types of prayers:

1. "I can handle it" prayer (passive activism)
2. "I can't handle it" prayer (active passivism)

"I can handle it" prayers are filled with announcements to God, petitions, and requests. We repeat ourselves with the idea that God will heal us if only we are faithful enough, pray enough, or find a secret word, phrase, or method to budge God our way. We ask him for things, but we do so in the context of having a plan for ourselves and our world. The unspoken undercurrent is control and self-reliance. We would never say so, but these kinds of prayers are really an attempt to use God as a vending machine. Insert the proper words and follow the right practice, and *then* God will answer the way we ask.

If we pray this way, it will lead to one of three results:

Denial: We assign positive outcomes to the quality of our prayers while ignoring all the prayers in the world (ours and other people's) that go contrary to our requests. Our transaction-based prayers require denial as part of the process.

Disillusionment: We become disillusioned by the lack of "results" and stop praying for a season, or maybe we walk away from prayer altogether.

Surrender: When we come to the end of this ritual method of prayer, it's transformed into something profound and true. This is the *I can't handle it* prayer.

True prayer, by definition, is an act of surrender—the antidote to grasping for control (and the anxiety produced by such striving). We don't have to live in denial or disillusionment; we only need to understand prayer as an act of surrender to our tender Abba, not as a means to control our world.

In his personal prayers to God, Jesus was actively passive. Notice his stance of surrender in the prayer he taught to his disciples:

Our Father in heaven, hallowed be your name. Your kingdom come, your will be done, on earth as it is in heaven. Give us this day our daily bread, and forgive us our debts, as we also have forgiven our debtors. And lead us not into temptation, but deliver us from evil.

MATTHEW 6:9-13

Jesus' prayer begins with the address "Father." From the first word, Jesus was saying, "You're my Father. You know best." Before presenting his concerns and needs, he said, "Your will be done." I have learned the hard way that trying to strong-arm God with our concerns only leaves us tired. But when we surrender our concerns to God, we find ourselves on a path of freedom and peace.

I used to feel regret over, and even shame myself about, my lack of prayer. But as my definition of prayer has expanded, I no longer think the only expression of prayer is sitting in a chair or bowing my head in my room. Prayer is any time the heart and the mind are moving toward surrender with God.

Prayer is relationship, not transaction. Surrendering prayer may be done in an air-conditioned office, on a path in the forest, or behind the wheel of a Toyota Camry while driving down the interstate. We can paint prayers, journal prayers, think prayers, feel prayers, and sing prayers. We can be silent in prayer and scream in prayer. We can worship in prayer and meditate on Scripture in prayer.

At its core, prayer is a relationship between us and our Abba, who loves us with grace upon grace and creates in us a heart that desires his presence more than a transaction with a vending machine in the sky.

Hoping for Change

SCOTTY'S WIFE, DARLENE, was twenty-four years old when her father was found dead by a bullet wound. She was told it was suicide at the time, but details that emerged after his death have prompted questions about whether he was murdered. She and Scotty had been married only a few years, and their first child was an infant. Neither Darlene nor Scotty knew how to navigate the barrage of grief, shock, sorrow, and ambivalence that came with his death. Over time her anger grew, as did Scotty's emotional distance.

Darlene had always been the peacemaker in her family, seeking to build bridges and reduce conflict among her parents and siblings. Her father's alcoholism created an unstable, unpredictable environment. After his death, the backstory of her life began to catch up with her. In the years following her father's death, Darlene began to suffer from post-traumatic stress as a result of the childhood trauma she'd endured. She spiraled into depression and anger.

Scotty loved her the best he knew how, but he was pretty clueless about how to enter and engage her pain. As a man of many words, he didn't know what to say about his young bride's great loss and new struggle with her faith. As for Darlene, she didn't know how to interpret Scotty's silence. It reminded her of the dysfunctional childhood family she came from, triggering her fear and anger. She lashed out at Scotty, only to have him withdraw emotionally or busy himself with more ministry.

Three years after her dad's death, Scotty and Darlene moved to Nashville. They had one child at the time, a three-year-old little girl, with a boy soon to arrive. This transition prompted Darlene to begin some much-needed reflection and counseling. As she gained insight into her story and new dimensions of God's healing grace, she begged Scotty to join her.

She told Scotty, "Honey, I'm not going anywhere. I'm with you, and I love you. But I'm committed to doing this heart work. I want to get healthy with you, but if you don't join me, I will continue to get healthy without you." She wasn't threatening Scotty; she was inviting him—beckoning him—to join her.

Darlene knew her pain was getting the best of her, robbing her of peace and contentment and causing suffering in those she loved most. In counseling, she found a safe place to look at her devastating childhood, the sexual abuse she'd endured, and the ways she and Scotty were living as hostages to their pain. Darlene and Scotty had both been orphaned in their family of origin, and they also lived like spiritual orphans—strangers to the greater dimensions of God's love in Jesus.

All through their marriage and ministry, Darlene prayed for Scotty, that he would have a breakthrough that would help him face his mom's death and connect with his dad and that he would have a more open heart toward her and their family. She knew he could have a better life and they could have a stronger relationship if he would confront his pain. But that would take time . . . and a work of God's Spirit.

When I sat in the barn listening to Scotty those years earlier, I didn't realize I was reaping the benefits of Darlene's long process of healing, as well as her faithful prayers and waiting for Scotty. I was a beneficiary of her courage to move toward healing when she hurt most and her bravery to stay with her husband as she hoped for greater healing for him and their relationship.

Scotty came into my life at the intersection of head knowledge of the gospel and my anxious heart. When I met Scotty, I knew about the freedom the gospel offered. I felt like I understood it; I could explain it. But my heart continued to be bound by anxiety and fear.

Through the power of the Holy Spirit, and with Scotty's help, I was coming to understand that grace isn't just about getting us out of a pinch; more than that, grace empowers and animates change in us. The gospel is when the firefighter who pulls you out of the fire is also the doctor who saves your life, the plastic surgeon who repairs your scars, the insurance agent who sends the money to rebuild, and the carpenter who builds your new home from the ground up.

The gospel is one-way love, without end. We are already loved, and because we are loved, we no longer have to live in fear. We no longer have to live reactively—posturing, pretending, and performing. The further good news is that even when we live reactively, we are still loved and still held firmly in the Abba's arms. The moments when we realize that we've returned to posturing, pretending, and performing are, in fact, evidence that we're moving from shallow Christianity into the richness of grace.

●　　●　　●

In the first year of our church, I self-published a novel. I'd written it years earlier and took a break from writing while forming our church. Then, shortly after the church launched, I returned to editing and publishing the book. The allegory is about our hearts—my heart—and the need for wild grace amid a world of demand. I entitled it *Adao's Dance*, since Adao is a version of Adam, or "man," and grace is the dance of freedom waiting for each of us.

Kristy and I planned two book release parties. The first was at a friend's large home in Atlanta. We invited many of our friends and family from the area to celebrate with us.

The day of the party, we ran errands, stocking up on drinks and hors d'oeuvres. Kristy and I arrived early and made sure the books were stacked perfectly and the drinks and food were prepared for our guests. The party started at seven.

Seven came and went.

A few people straggled in.

We'd invited one hundred people. Where were they?

Be a pro, I told myself. I put on my professional pastor/writer face and delivered my book talk. No one knew I was upset.

When the party ended and the final few people left, Kristy and I began cleaning up. I moved swiftly and silently, packing up the leftover books, drinks, and food. I made a thousand trips to the car with a million thoughts taking my mind hostage: what I could have done better to prepare for the night, how I could have promoted the gathering better. I tried to gain perspective but couldn't.

Kristy and I pulled out of the driveway and drove through the familiar Atlanta streets toward the expressway. I began to feel a pain in the side of my neck—sharp, with an ache that dropped down through my shoulder and to my chest. I knew it wasn't a heart attack, but it hurt. I massaged my neck and chest with my right hand, steering with my left.

"Are you upset?" Kristy asked.

"I'm fine."

"There weren't many people there. It's okay to be upset," she said. "You can be disappointed. I'm disappointed."

"I know people are busy. I mean, we skip events all the time. I love skipping events." I smiled. We both knew this was true.

"You're still allowed to be upset," she said.

"Okay, I'm upset."

"It means a lot to you. And some friends and family weren't there to share it with you. People are the worst," she said with a gentle laugh.

"I don't even want to do the party in Marietta tomorrow night."

"We're doing it, and people will be there," she said. "Russ, I don't care. I think it's incredible what you've done. And I agree, tonight didn't meet our expectations. But I love you. I would love you even if you'd never written this story. Even if you never write a thing again in your life."

The pain in my neck eased, and the ache in my chest filled with warmth. My breath deepened into my lungs. On that drive, as we headed toward I-75, Kristy's love had the power to change me, moving me from despair to acceptance to peace.

Courage arrived where only discouragement had been operating.

Love has this ability.

We drive across the country to be with someone who loves us. We work three jobs for our children. We sleep hunched in a hospital chair, just in case she wakes up. Love changes everything. And that's just human love. Now imagine a love that's perfect and never failing, regardless of anything you do or don't do, say or don't say, think or don't think.

Love begets change.

It's not the other way around—God's love is not a result of our transformed lives. The voice of God may create awareness of sin, and may convict us, but the voice of God does not condemn or belittle us. In that freedom and peace, we are empowered to ask ourselves why we are doing the harmful things we do.

Why do I seek people's approval?
Why am I acting out or raging or hiding?
Why do I try to control everything?
Why am I addicted to work?
Why can't I shake this sense of shame or judgment—toward myself or someone else?

As Scotty tells me often, "We are fully free and also not as free as God intends us to be."

When we know that the Abba already loves us, we don't have to pretend anymore. This may be slow work, but as we surrender to it, we grow in our awareness of who God has already deemed us to be. We haven't arrived, but we're moving into the grace that washes over us with furious love.

From Scotty
Prayerful Contemplation

1. What contexts in life have reinforced the lie that we are what we achieve? Sports, academics, economics, romance, religion, family of origin, vocation, or something else?

2. When do you tend to feel most peaceful? Most anxious? Most fearful?

3. How do you see a "grace allergy" playing out in your life? What is at the root of your struggle to accept God's great love for you in Jesus?

4. Who in your life models contentment, peace, and having the right "price tags" in terms of their priorities?

5. What does your schedule reveal about your view of God, relationships, and what really matters?

THE FOURTH CONVERSATION

SUFFERING IS
A TEACHER.

From Scotty

I Was Eleven

IN OCTOBER OF 1961, about a week before my mom's accident and death, I dreamed that something terrible was going to happen to her. I didn't wake up in the middle of the night with the sights and sounds of a car wreck, and it didn't feel real enough to move me to tell Mom about it the next morning. I probably chalked up the experience to the general sadness I always felt if Mom left in the morning before I had a chance to tell her goodbye. The thought of life without her was a nightmare.

Premonitions, like dreams, are hard to put in a tidy biblical box. Over the years, I've encountered Christians who have shown more excitement and confidence in their dreams and visions than in God's Word itself—something that always turned me off and jaded my openness to personal spiritual encounters. Yet the Scriptures do affirm the reality of dreams and visions. (See Acts 2:17; 9:10; 16:9-10; 18:9.)

So what are we to make of these experiences? Are they

warnings from God or human impressions looking for a narrative to fulfill them? Or maybe they're just replays of a scene from a television show, a bit of undigested supper, or our imagination's way of expressing trauma and subliminal fears while we sleep. It's a mystery to me.

I never struggled with guilt over my silence about my dream, hunch, premonition, vision—whatever it was. But it does linger as a haunting part of my story. Should I have said something to her? Would it have made any difference?

My theology tells me otherwise, because our days, like our hairs, are numbered by God. I am thankful to know that God is absolutely sovereign over all things. I don't think that makes us robots, but it does mean God is great. The older I've gotten, the more I happily hold sovereignty and mystery together.

Though I wasn't responsible for Mom's death, I was responsible for dealing with how her death impacted me. Unfortunately, I waited forty years to deal with it.

Entering Suffering

"WE ALL HAVE PAIN," Scotty told me. "My pain has been stockpiling with interest as a result of sexual abuse at age eight, the death of my mom when I was eleven, the death of a girlfriend at eighteen, and then the perpetual emotional absence of my dad."

We were in the church he had once led and now hangs around as a mentor. We were holed up in a conference room on the second floor where no one could find us. I wasn't sure what to say to Scotty about his abuse. He had mentioned it to me only once before, without any detail or reflection.

"Is being abused something you talk about?" I asked hesitantly. "We don't have to talk about it if you don't want to."

"It's okay. It's something I didn't begin talking about until recently, even though it was part of my healing process. My abuse wasn't episodic, but a horrible incident involving a neighbor and pornography and unwanted touch," he said.

"What did that trauma do to you as a boy?"

"As a child, I heard the mantra 'Big boys don't cry.' I got the message that sadness and pain were not okay, so I hid. Now I understand the trauma as a violation of God's image inside me, a violation of how the world should work."

"How do you react to that trauma now that you're not hiding?" I asked.

"I try to validate the pain and sit in it rather than hide from it. Letting myself feel sadness has been an important part of my healing. I used to fear that if I really started grieving, I might never stop. We experience trauma not just as a result of the bad things that happen but also as a result of the good things that didn't happen. Being ignored can be just as traumatic as being abused. Not all of us have stories of horrible events, but we all have real stories of pain."

This felt like a revelation for me, and I sat there trying to take it all in.

"We become more real by entering suffering, not running from it," he went on. "I had to acknowledge the abuse, loss, and neglect . . . and the pain associated with each. The world—even Christian subculture—wants us to move on, get over it, busy ourselves with something more productive. But that's not the way of the gospel."

Finally I asked, "What should we do?"

"Russ, most people have a reservoir of undealt-with grief. I was fifty years old when I began to acknowledge and grieve my abuse, to grieve any of my pain. It's good news that people can deal with trauma and pain at any age, but do it now. Don't wait. I wish I'd grieved Mom so much sooner. *Much* sooner."

Later, as I reflected on my conversation with Scotty, it struck me that suffering comes not just in the original event but also in the reaction to the event. In the face of grief, my tendency was to stay busy. I thought I was doing myself a favor by moving away from the pain, but I was only causing more pain—anxiety, relational distance, negativity—by repressing it.

The Psalms provide a healthier alternative for the soul in turmoil: the opportunity to preach hope to ourselves. Psalm 42:5-6 puts it this way: "Why are you cast down, O my soul, and why are you in turmoil within me? Hope in God; for I shall again praise him, my salvation and my God." The psalmist is processing his pain by speaking to himself about and in and through that pain. As he addresses his soul's current state or mood, he demonstrates that while his soul is affected by pain, he isn't defined by it.

When we recognize that pain is only a part of our story, we can speak hope in the face of suffering. Not only that, but we have a God who is with us in our suffering. The great band R.E.M. sings, "Everybody hurts,"[1] but the reality is that while everybody hurts, not everybody hopes in the hurt. Usually our hope is defined by uncertainty.

I *hope* the field goal kick goes in to win the game.

I *hope* I win the lottery.

I *hope* she loves me.

But biblical hope is different. It's an expectation of something to happen in the certainty of God. Our hope can be certain because it isn't attached to a particular outcome but to God himself.

Paul helps us make sense of the kind of hope created in the wake of suffering: "We rejoice in our sufferings, knowing that suffering produces endurance, and endurance produces character, and character produces hope, and hope does not put us to shame, because God's love has been poured into our hearts through the Holy Spirit who has been given to us" (Romans 5:3-5).

Paul isn't telling us to rejoice in the event of suffering itself. Paul is saying that suffering can be a teacher, guiding us toward endurance, character, and hope. In some mysterious way, hope is being born in the face of pain. So rejoice. The story is not over.

And even as we grieve the pain, we can be comforted by our steady joy in Christ, who never changes, who is all sufficient, who suffered himself, and who promises to wipe away every tear from every eye.

Facing Grief

WE CELEBRATED our church's first Easter as a core group of twenty adults and dozens of kids at a park in our town. At the time, we didn't own a building or even have leased space; we were meeting in someone's living room on Sunday mornings. So it made the most sense to be outside in the spring morning, sharing breakfast, letting our children play, singing, and hearing the Resurrection story together.

We set up food in a gazebo and gathered around on picnic blankets and in chairs. I stood and read the story of Christ's resurrection and spoke about the good news of victory on the other side of death. My friend Jason sat to my right in a metal lawn chair. I remember him sitting with his legs crossed, smiling in the sun.

This is the Jason I choose to remember.

Jason's son and daughter were playing on the playground behind us. He had recently been through a divorce and was looking for a church home where he could have a fresh start. He had been part of our little launch group for the previous four months. Jason was friendly, kind, and eager to learn and help. I liked him right away.

A promising young business owner in our town, Jason reviewed our first lease on a building and helped us file legal papers. He even researched the plat on the home I purchased to make sure everything was just right for Kristy and the girls and me. Jason and I talked a lot about our kids, about trying to be a good dad, about brushing tangles out of our daughters' hair at night. We would grab sandwiches at the local café, and I would listen to his regret, pain, and loneliness.

Then one day my phone rang.

"Jason killed himself last night," my friend Allen told me.

"I don't think I heard you," I said. "Can you repeat that?" I walked out of the house and into the warm Florida air. It was spring break, and my family was gathered at my in-laws' house in Orlando.

"I need you to repeat that," I said again.

"I'm sorry. Jason killed himself last night."

"Allen, I know it is April 1. That's not funny."

"It's not a joke. Jason killed himself last night at his house. I don't know anything more than that," Allen said. "What do we do?"

I didn't know what to do. I'd never led anyone through losing a key member of a church, not to mention losing a friend, a father, an ex-husband, a child, or a sibling. This was a loss not only to Jason's family and friends but also to his coworkers and our whole town.

At my previous church, I was insulated; the congregational care office would handle something like this, not me. I called Jake, my church-planting coach, and asked what I should do.

He calmly replied, "You come home immediately."

I sat my children down on the couch and told them something

horrible had happened—that someone had died and we had to drive through the night so I could be there to help in the morning.

The truth is, I didn't want to go home. I wanted to stay hidden in Florida and avoid it all. Maybe the trauma for Jason's family and friends, and even inside me, would go away with enough geographical distance.

We drove through the night, and Kristy took notes on a sheet of paper as I talked through what I would say at Jason's business in the morning. The trip took seven hours, and eventually Kristy began to doze in the darkness. I was numb, but underneath that I could feel twitches of anger, confusion, and sadness.

The loss triggered my heart and mind to other losses. Loss and hurt from my childhood. The unborn baby Kristy and I had lost before any of our daughters were born. Broken relationships. The loss of good things I had expected to come our way. As the grief rose up inside me, I packed all the emotions into boxes, filing them away deep in my heart.

I gripped the steering wheel and kept driving.

◦   ◦   ◦

The next day I spoke in a crowded conference room to Jason's friends and coworkers. For many people there, this was the first time they'd heard the news, and their faces were empty, their hearts ripped wide open. I tried my best to honor Jason and his life, his work, and his children, despite the horrific, permanent decision he'd made the previous night.

One moment doesn't define a person, I said.

I told them I didn't understand why this had happened, but I did know that God loved Jason without measure amid all the pain he must have been feeling.

I drove the few blocks to Jason's house and went inside to meet Jason's mom and dad. Somewhere else, in a neighboring town, his children and ex-wife were trying to process this tragic loss and grief. I glanced around the room. On a table beside Jason's recliner, I saw a devotional book and a picture of his kids. His passport and some papers were laid out on the dining room table, prepared for an upcoming trip to Guatemala he'd been planning to take with me and a group of guys.

His parents and I talked about the funeral, taking turns leaving the room when we fell into uncontrolled weeping. Only once did I look down the hall and into Jason's bedroom where the police had draped a white sheet over his bed. I couldn't help but imagine him sitting alone on his bed, contemplating his fatal decision.

I wondered how long he'd sat there. I wondered if he moved around the house, trying to walk off the urge. I wondered if he prayed. I wondered if he thought about calling anyone for help. I was seized by a wave of guilt. *Why didn't I reach out to him more? Why didn't he call me?* I kept asking myself.

I led Jason's funeral and then began to process all the pain and confusion with his friends, who were hurting and had questions. I knew nothing about grief, so I found myself in a crash course about both suicide and grieving. The journey through grief is long and chaotic and nonlinear, and it looks different for each person. We have to cycle through a wide range of reactions—denial, anger, bargaining, and depression—before we can come to terms with what happened (the acceptance stage).

It's a long road before our hearts can say, "Okay."

We'd rather stay busy—buy something, experience something, be happy, judge someone else—than face our loss and pain.

I can see now that this has been my pattern with pain since the eighth grade, when my parents divorced and my grandfather died. I found that by being friendly and using humor, I could fit in—even win friends and be popular. And if I did, I wouldn't have to feel the pain.

●　　●　　●

Throughout high school, I not only didn't allow myself to feel any of my emotional pain, I avoided the discussion of it altogether. In college, during reflective moments, usually in worship settings, I would fight back the reservoir of pain and emotion that would surface. I sometimes acknowledged the pain, but I wasn't ready to feel it. I immersed myself in schoolwork and activities so I could avoid the negative feelings I'd packed away.

I feared grief.

I feared sadness.

I didn't mask my sadness with anger, just a busy heart. But with Jason's death, I was discovering that pain doesn't go away unless you face it and feel it. It may hide and shift, but it always resurfaces.

When Scotty and I became friends, I was just beginning the process of facing pain. Scotty confirmed what I was learning.

"I had to feel the impact of it all," he told me. "I had to feel the loss and pain in the presence of a God who didn't shame me but loved me. That was when the healing began."

"So you went forty years without facing your defining pain?" I asked.

"I had a lot of undealt-with grief," he said. "I was fifty, at a place of utter mental, physical, and emotional exhaustion, when I began to process my mom's death. The very place I'd been avoiding was the place my heart began to thaw out. As I risked loving and trusting other people, I experienced a kind of joy and comfort I'd never known before."

"What did that look like?" I asked.

"I needed to see that the Bible never condemns our feelings. I'd grown up in this world where things like anger or melancholy were seen as the absence of God's blessing. I used to avoid the passages in Scripture, especially certain psalms, that show deep anguish or anger. In reality, those psalms are a gift. I needed to feel the sadness and not be in a hurry. I needed to give myself grace in my grief, to weep more and sit longer with the Lord. I needed to know he was with me and could handle my pain."

I knew the time was arriving—a disruption of grace into my boxed-up and filed-away grief. It was time for me to slow down and wade into the healing waters of God.

$$\circ \quad \circ \quad \circ$$

From Scotty
My Dad

Dad lied about his age in order to enlist in the Navy during World War II. At the age of seventeen, without finishing high school, he went to sea. When I look at seventeen-year-olds today, I'm shocked at how young they look—how young he was. I'm also filled with admiration for what Dad accomplished.

Near the end of Dad's life, I discovered that his rush to join the Navy was more about running from the war of his home life than wanting to do his part in the war. His childhood in Danville, Virginia, was marked by poverty and abuse. The Navy was his way out, and it birthed in him a love for big water and an endless wanderlust.

After several years in the Navy during World War II, my dad and a buddy decided to hitchhike to Los Angeles with the hope of heading north and joining the Royal Canadian Air Force. I never got all the details about that failed adventure, but while he was in California, Dad found out the Merchant Marine was looking for new candidates to enter the officer training ranks. He took the GED and was accepted into the Merchant Marine Academy in Los Angeles.

Dad became a navigator in the early radar days, which meant he learned to read the stars and planets with a sextant—guiding huge ships across the globe using ocean charts, complex trigonometry, dead reckoning, and some serious courage.

◎　　◎　　◎

In June of 1962, I was twelve years old. It was the summer after Mom died, and Dad took me on a road trip to Fort Lauderdale, Florida, while my brother stayed home for football practice. He didn't mention why we were going to Florida, but soon we were visiting yacht clubs, sea docks, and boat sellers. For a brief season, Dad considered buying a yacht, perhaps moving to the coast and introducing his two boys to his love for the ocean.

The trip offered a glimpse beyond the disconnect I usually felt with Dad, but soon enough the adventure ended, and we returned to North Carolina, where the storm of Mom's death took Dad deeper into grief and depression.

But I still have those four days. I got a glimpse of the dad he might have been, a glimpse of how hope could have sustained our family through our suffering. Our family suffered not just the pain and loss of my mom but the long-term deterioration of our relationships with each other.

I didn't want to follow that same pattern for my life. I needed to find a better way.

Hope in the Darkness

I RECENTLY HEARD an interview with Stephen Colbert, anchor of *The Late Show*, on *Anderson Cooper 360*. He talked about the loss of his father and two brothers, who died in a plane crash when Colbert was ten years old. Anderson Cooper's mother, Gloria Vanderbilt, had recently passed away at the time of the interview, and his father, like Colbert's, had died when he was ten. Cooper said it felt like the trajectory of his life was altered by the loss of his dad, like time was forever marked by the event.

Cooper said to Colbert, "You told an interviewer that you have learned to—in your words—'love the thing that I most wish had not happened.'"

Cooper began to tear up and paused to regain control of his breathing.

Cooper continued, "You went on to say, 'What punishments of God are not gifts?' Do you really believe that?"

"Yes," Colbert replied. Then he quoted from Tolkien's *The*

Lord of the Rings: "'It's a gift to exist, and with existence comes suffering.' There's no escaping that. . . . I don't want it to have happened. I want it to *not* have happened, but if you are grateful for your life—which I think is a positive thing to do, not everybody is, and I am not always, but it's the most positive thing to do—then you have to be grateful for all of it. You can't pick and choose what you're grateful for."

Colbert then pondered what we get from loss, concluding, "You get awareness of other people's loss, which allows you to connect with that other person, which allows you to love more deeply and to understand what it's like to be a human being if it's true that all humans suffer. . . . At a young age, I suffered something so that by the time I was in serious relationships in my life, with friends, or with my wife, or with my children, I'm understanding that everyone is suffering."[2]

While I don't think of all suffering as "punishments of God," I do think those experiences are gifts to the extent that they teach us about our great God and give us the opportunity to find solace in him.

I've always found the story in John 11 difficult to accept, but it also offers some insight into our own suffering. Jesus was told by two sisters, Mary and Martha, that their brother, Lazarus, was dying. Jesus deeply loved all three of them. But after being told about his friend Lazarus's condition, Jesus delayed. Then Lazarus died.

In other words, Jesus let his friend die.

Jesus held the power to heal Lazarus, yet he decided not to exercise his power in the way we suppose he should have. When

Jesus finally arrived, Martha approached him. "Lord," she said, "if you had been here, my brother would not have died. But I know that even now God will give you whatever you ask" (see John 11:21-22, NIV).

She was respectfully saying, "I hate what you did. I don't get it. But my faith in you is still here. You can fix this."

Mary arrived next. "When Mary reached the place where Jesus was and saw him, she fell at his feet and said, 'Lord, if you had been here, my brother would not have died'" (John 11:32, NIV). Mary was saying, "I don't understand. I don't get it. Why weren't you here?"

Jesus gave her—and us—something greater than an explanation. As she broke down weeping, Jesus gave her compassion.

Jesus wept with her.

I often think I need a detailed explanation of why something happened to me or those around me. I assume another book on the sovereignty of God or some wisdom about the will of God from a respected theologian will finally satisfy my inability to grasp God's role in our suffering.

But explanation does not heal.

We need presence in pain; we need the constant God who comforts those who have been broken, just as he was broken. God never promises explanation, but he does promise his presence.

Perhaps the most significant place of God's revelation to humankind is not through glory but suffering: God himself experiencing the pain of the Cross. The Cross—the image of Christ's torture, pain, and brokenness—reminds us that his love conquered everything, even death. And that love reaches to all the places we go and all the feelings we experience.

In the evenings I tuck my daughters in their bed and pray for them. I often ask them, "Who made you?"

They respond, "God."

"And what is God?"

"Love."

"And when does he love you?"

"All the time."

"All the time," I repeat.

And I pray for them. Of course, I don't pray for suffering for them, but I do pray they would learn to be honest about the hurt in their hearts. My hope for my girls as they walk through a world filled with suffering is that they know that God is with them just as much in their suffering as he is in the rainbow-and-lollipop moments of their lives.

That's also the hope I hold for myself.

Loyal Love

I OPERATED ROBOTICALLY the week after Jason killed himself. Throughout the following month, as I hosted groups in my home and met with people one-on-one, allowing them to relive the loss, I listened to their feelings of confusion, anger, and sadness. But I led from behind the curtain.

I thought if I knew how Jason did it, I would be settled. If only I knew his movements that final day. If I could just find out about his communications. If I learned more about him than I knew before. I was playing a game of control in an attempt to avoid pain. I thought if I could explain this, I wouldn't have to feel it.

If I could explain it, I wouldn't have to face the loss and hurt.

Some explanation did come in time. It helped me understand Jason as a person, and it allowed me to see the depth of emotional pain he was experiencing but largely kept to himself. I learned what he did that final day—who he called, what emails he sent. I learned about some kind words he left behind and some that caused more pain. The details helped me understand, but they didn't help me heal. My confusion left, but my sadness remained.

Without realizing it, I took on emotional weight from friends and people in our church who were hurting. I internally pledged to be steady and strong through the storm. I grew numb to emotion and more exhausted by the day.

A month after Jason's death, I had lunch with a retired friend, Greg, who was a member at the church where I used to work. Greg was a former logistics specialist at Home Depot corporate, so he loved to inquire about the systems and backup systems and backup, backup systems we were developing in our church. He would kindly ask, "What happens if you get sick Saturday night? What are the simple steps for someone to get to know other people? What happens if the power goes out in the building? What happens if the HVAC breaks?"

He would then smirk and nod, "Okay, sounds like you thought about that." About every tenth question, he would come upon a detail I hadn't thought of yet. I would make a note of it and have it fixed by our next lunch. This method of systematic interrogation was incredibly valuable as we got our church off the ground. But this lunch was different.

"You look horrible," Greg said to me when we were seated in our booth.

"One of our guys killed himself last month," I said bluntly.

"Oh, I'm sorry." Greg was quiet for a moment, taking in the shock.

"He was one of the first men in our church," I said. "He helped us get started."

"You look like you don't have anything left," he said. "I can see it in your face. I've never seen you look like this."

He hadn't seen me for a few months, so he clearly saw the before and after. Everybody else in my life was either going through the same trauma or walking with me on an ongoing basis. But he saw a spade and called it a spade.

"It feels like I've just been pouring myself out ever since," I said.

"Is that your plan from this point on?"

"What do you mean? That's my job. I have to lead through those heart-wrenching conversations and maintain my composure. I had to plan the funeral and preach it and not be an emotional wreck the entire time."

"I know that's your job," he said, "but you can't do your job if you aren't taken care of. You need a break, or you're going to crash."

He didn't say any more. He didn't advise me on how to rest or refuel, nor did he give me a counseling session on grief. He didn't try to dig out the compartmentalized sadness boxed away in my heart. He just helped me see reality. I'd walked my church and community through trauma for a month straight and had yet to process how I felt about it.

I was headed toward emotional collapse.

◎　　◎　　◎

My walks in the woods grew longer, and rather than consuming my mind with how everybody else was doing, I permitted myself to feel what I was feeling. I would talk to Jason in my car as I drove around our town. At first these conversations were angry. Sometimes I called him names or cussed at him. At other times the conversations reflected my confusion, asking him the many whys.

This helped for a while—at least I was getting my emotions

out. Eventually, however, the conversations became statements of my sadness. As I spoke, I grew aware of the Compassionate Presence who is with us in our sadness. Healing began to take place in my heart, and the conversations became statements of compassion toward Jason as I recognized the deep sadness he must have been carrying.

There were other conversations I had with God on those walks and drives. Weary yet bold, I finally stated out loud the feelings hidden in my heart.

God, I think it's cruel and ridiculous that people die in such excruciating ways.
I'm struggling with why depression and mental illness are a part of your world.
Why do children go to bed weeping, without a mom or dad?
Why do families break? Why do people break?
Breakthrough doesn't always happen like it does in fairy tales.
Waves come ashore from your oceans and drown your children. Your oceans!
I think all of this is rubbish.

I dared to speak what my heart actually felt, trusting that God's loyal love would hold me and lead me. I longed to rest deeper in the vision of a day when there is no winter but only spring, when pain is fully restored, when the sadness of this world is transformed into eternal gladness.

Making Wounds Sacred

It was evening, a time my friend Jeremy normally wouldn't have called, and I normally wouldn't have picked up.

"Holly is missing," he said. "No one can find her. Last we heard, she drove up toward their cabin in the mountains. Let me know if you hear anything, and please pray for her and the family."

An image of her smiling in her kitchen, holding one of her children on her hip, flashed in my mind. Then came images of all of her children and her husband and images of my wife laughing with her.

My wife loved Holly.

All I could think was, *Please, no. Not again.*

Holly was one of Kristy's best friends. We had met Holly and her family at our church in Atlanta when Kristy was in a mom's group with her. When we had our first daughter, Holly and Matt already had three. Holly taught Kristy how to grocery shop with a little one and not be miserable. "Give yourself grace and time," she said.

Holly taught Kristy about prepping and cooking meals, about eating well and creating a healthy food environment for children. She was one of an elite handful of moms Kristy admired, befriended, and asked the millions of questions a new mother has rattling around in her head.

From the moment Kristy and I began talking about starting a church, Holly and Matt supported us. They told us they wished they lived near us so they could come every week, and they sent checks to support us when we didn't have enough to support ourselves.

I waited until we finished tucking the girls into their beds to tell Kristy that Holly was missing. The next day we learned she had killed herself.

⊙　　⊙　　⊙

I think back to our Easter service at the park and the twenty adults sitting around in the sunshine. Jason was sitting in his lawn chair, smiling, and Holly was a few lawn chairs over with her husband, their daughters, and their baby boy. They had driven up from Atlanta to be with our little church on our first Easter together.

And now, just two years later, Jason and Holly were no longer with us in this life.

Kristy helped organize the funeral, and I gave a personal reflection about Holly at the service. Kristy numbed the pain by going into helper mode. She spent the next month driving back and forth to Atlanta to help Holly's husband and a few friends unpack and organize their new home, as they'd moved just a week prior to the tragedy.

Then came her anger.

How could Holly just leave us?
How could she leave her children?
Her husband?
I know she loved them!
What did I miss?
Why didn't she call when she needed help?

Then came Kristy's sadness.

Things that once mattered to her no longer mattered. I knew enough from Jason's death to give her grace and time. Holly's own advice: *grace and time.*

I wish Jason and Holly both could have taken in those three words.

I also knew the best thing I could do for Kristy was to encourage her to keep talking. So on Thursday evenings we would drive to Atlanta to our favorite restaurant and wait in line for margaritas and tacos. We'd find a table on the patio and talk.

"Have you been thinking about her a lot this week?" I asked.

"I just keep cycling through my texts with her, trying to see what I missed," Kristy said. "Russ, she texted me *that morning.*"

"And you can't figure out why she didn't say anything," I said.

"Right, nothing. She said nothing to me. And I love her."

"She loved you," I said.

"Then she drove away. She said nothing. How could she say nothing?"

"I guess she was trying to hold it all together, and then the dam broke."

"She was baking muffins that morning!" Kristy vented. "I

cleaned her kitchen the next day, and she was halfway through baking muffins when she left. Muffins, Russ!"

"How much are you thinking about that day—the day you walked into her house?"

"I think about it a lot. The beautiful home and those lovely children. She loved her kids. And then I create what it must have been like for her trying to outrun her urge to kill herself. I wish she would have called. I just want her back," Kristy said. "I'm so tired."

Kristy and I listened to podcasts about grief. We read books. We kept talking. There was no other way. We were at our end, and we had to feel all the pain, all the loss.

Slowly, over the course of months, Kristy came out of her depression and was simply and utterly sad. This didn't happen in one specific moment on one particular day, but over time I began to see her smiling in the sun more frequently than drowning in the sea of sorrow. What was once an active wound started becoming a sacred place of healing. Where there had been trauma and despair, there was a place of love, compassion, and new life.

As I watched Kristy's resolve to grieve Holly in a healthy way, I was forced to face my own pain—not just the loss of Jason and Holly but also the grief from my past. If Jason's death cracked open the door to see the reservoir of pain within, Holly's death pushed me into the reservoir completely. I was beginning to understand it wasn't just the big horrors of suffering that I was feeling but also the millions of "small" sufferings from everyday life that I had no skill set to grieve. I was learning that all pain and loss, as well as all change (both good and bad)—from moving to changing jobs to child-rearing to aging—has to be grieved, or the sadness will never heal.

The only way I have found to heal is to rest in this: *God is love.* When we trust his character and sovereignty, we believe he will carry us through, buoying us in our grief and suffering, sustaining us in joy and in sorrow.

"Sovereignty is comforting not because it gives me answers," Scotty said, "but because it gives me God."

I held on to those words of Scotty's like a lifeline.

◉   ◉   ◉

One summer morning I sat with a couple from our church who had just received the news that their little boy's tumor was benign. But the doctors also told them their son had a rare, incurable disease in which tumors, benign or malignant, could randomly grow in his body at any time. They were told this may mean his future would be filled with tumors and cancer treatments or it may mean his preexisting tumor would never grow and he would never get another tumor.

In other words, they were powerless.

Their new normal included uncertainty and periodic MRIs for the rest of their son's life. I prayed for the couple and for their child—for his body, for the doctors, and most of all, for their hearts.

Afterward, I got in my truck and drove south toward Atlanta for a lunch meeting. The sun was bright, traffic was light, and I drove freely, my heart and mind wandering. I thought about the fear my friends had to face, the fear their son would know as normal. I thought about the loss they may experience in that fear. I thought about the losses I'd experienced throughout life and the active wounds in my life that needed healing.

How could Kristy and I have miscarried a baby and I never cried?
I wondered.

*How hard must my heart have been to listen to my wife suffer in the
bathroom an entire night miscarrying a baby, and I never shed a tear?*

I didn't realize the consequences of my unaddressed pain: my
lack of empathy, my lack of tenderness, my tendency to withdraw.

But a thaw was beginning in my heart—I could feel it.

I called Scotty and told him about my meeting with the couple.
"What is sovereignty?" I asked him.

"For me, months shy of my seventieth birthday, the sovereignty of God is far more about having a heavenly Father I can
trust rather than a theological category I need to defend. Through
the gospel, I've come to know God as all-powerful, all-loving, and
utterly trustworthy. But he can't be domesticated, and he isn't
predictable or manageable. I am more certain than ever of his
great love for us in Jesus, but I'm equally more at home in the
mystery of his ways and timing."

I could hear the wind rustling through his phone, and Scotty
was out of breath. I knew he was walking around his neighborhood, getting his steps in for the day.

"What would it mean for an active wound to become sacred?"
I asked.

"I love those words, Russ. Something becomes sacred when
it's seen in another light and set apart. It may be the same wound,
but it looks different in light of our belovedness. For instance, as
a son or daughter of God, I'm invited to not despise my weakness
but boast in it."

"What does it mean to boast in weakness?" I asked.

"I boast in my weakness to the degree that I boast in Christ. That is, I am at home in him—I rest in his mercy, grace, and love for me. The weakness of Jesus' Cross saved me. Jesus was the quintessential sufferer, familiar with grief. It's a holy paradox, but a true paradox."

Scotty caught his breath and continued. "The more we come alive to the riches of the gospel, the more we bring our trauma and woundedness to our Father. He doesn't despise our weakness and suffering, so neither should we. Our wounds need to be embraced as a part of our story—not defining us, but driving us deeper into love for God and compassion for fellow sufferers. Most of us deny our wounds out of fear of being weak or damaged. But our greatest need isn't for relief from our pain but for changed hearts."

"And then we are emotionally healed?" I asked.

"Healing isn't past tense, Russ. It's a lifelong journey. An emotionally healthy person is someone who is coming alive to the broad range of feelings that accompany being sinner-saints. Right now, God loves us as much as he will ever love us. But we won't be completely healthy and whole until the return of Jesus. The great news is, our Father will complete the good work he has begun in us. The challenging news is, the more we grow, the more of our brokenness and weakness we will discover. All of this, of course, makes Jesus even more essential and precious to us."

"So is healing simply being in the process of becoming healthier?" I asked.

"Yeah, I can go with that. A big part of our healing happens instantaneously when God reconciles us to himself through the finished work of Jesus. That is a once-and-for-all healing. The

Bible calls that gracious act of God justification. God declares us to be eternally forgiven and perfectly righteous in Christ. But our justification launches us into a lifelong journey of becoming like Jesus—perfectly whole, free, healthy."

I tried to let all that soak in. I had known the gospel for years, yet Scotty was leading me on a journey of resting fully in my belovedness *and* receiving transformative implications of that gift.

"We need forgiveness *and* healing. But the pressure is off. We are loved fully and perfectly now, so we can stay in the process of becoming healthier without anxiety, fear, or pride. God doesn't love us to the extent we are like Jesus—healthy, whole, and loving—but to the degree we are *in* Jesus, which is 100 percent."

From Scotty
Prayerful Contemplation

1. What messages did you get early in life about pain and suffering? For example: "Big boys don't cry," "Suck it up," "Get over it," or "God would never allow suffering in your life if he loves you—you must be at fault." (What a pernicious lie.)

2. What models did you have for dealing with pain? Were there people in your life who dealt with grief in a healthy way? Were there others who taught you to deal with pain by living in denial or medicating it in ineffective ways? (This isn't an exercise in blame but in recognizing some patterns than need to be identified and broken.)

3. What kind of suffering do you fear the most—physical, relational, financial? Who or what has reinforced the fear of suffering in your life?

4. How has suffering proven to be a trustworthy teacher in your life? What have you learned from pain you couldn't learn any other way?

5. The Bible says that Jesus' resurrection body will bear the marks of his suffering forever. What is the significance of this to us? If we will know him by his scars, why do we despise our own scars?

VULNERABILITY IS ESSENTIAL FOR HEALING AND CONNECTION.

Ending Up Lonely

"TELL ME ABOUT THE TRIP." I was talking to Scotty on my way to Target. I knew he'd just returned from a fishing trip with friends to Canada, and I was eager to hear his stories.

"It was fantastic. We went to this remote lake—you would love it there. We stayed on a couple of houseboats anchored in a cove, and we took fishing boats out each day. At night we cooked our fish and sipped expensive bourbon—one guy actually owns a brand of bourbon! We told stories and sat under the stars."

"Who was there?" I asked.

"One guy puts the trip together, and a handful of friends always go. These are guys I've been journeying with for a long time. Some gospel posse guys."

Scotty and I are both introverts by nature, so when I was first getting to know him, I was struck by how much he invested in the people around him. His life wasn't just about work; he seemed to strike a balance between faith, work, *and* relationships. Sure, he was somewhat retired, but he still had plenty of work opportunities to accept if he desired. Nonetheless, for every couple of work trips on the calendar, there was a trip to the beach with Darlene, a day watching his grandkids, or a fishing trip with his friends.

"Have you always had a group of friends?" I asked. "I mean, when you were my age—midcareer, with family and so many demands?"

"Loneliness is a big deal, Russ," he said. "Everybody experiences loneliness, but as we grow into our belovedness, as we come more alive to God's great love for us in Jesus, we become better equipped to face it and deal with it."

"So what do we do?"

As always, I wanted a formula, a firm plan.

"The goal isn't to get over loneliness but to steward it—to recognize when our feelings of loneliness are more connected to our default mode of isolation and withdrawal than anything else. It's a paradox, but sometimes the answer to toxic loneliness is to spend time alone with Jesus. You and I are introverts—the goal isn't for us to become extroverts. It's to know Jesus better so that when we're with people, they experience his kindness, not our competence."

"Why is it so hard for me to build rewarding friendships?" I asked. "And why is it so hard for me to admit I'm lonely?"

"Our culture promotes loneliness by selling us on opportunities for fake intimacy. It pushes us toward paths of escape and performance that temporarily make us feel connected. But these imitations don't require the emotional risk necessary for real connection."

"So loneliness is a trick we buy into?" I asked.

"In a way. In our loneliness, we hold on to our secrets because we think we can't risk telling someone how we feel or being known in general. So we settle for the illusion of connection and end up with alienation, even addiction. For example, pornography can only give us the illusion of being desired. We think we're getting a little of what we want—connection and intimacy—without paying the price of genuine intimacy and the messiness of relationship. It's counterfeit connection."

◉   ◉   ◉

After almost a decade of living in Atlanta, Kristy and I had a tight group of friends. When I worked at the big church, my office was just down the hall from my friends. I sat next to them in meetings, celebrated with them, and complained to them, over lunch. We benefited from the bonds of friendship and quality time without any awareness of the ease of the gift.

But once we started our new church, Kristy and I had no structure in place for seeing our friends. We happily settled into our new town and began meeting kind, friendly people. I became hyperfocused on the church and our family, and in the pursuit of these good things, I neglected some other key parts of my life. I had begun to disregard my dearest friends.

My new life was about trying to start something, which was certainly intoxicating, but the day-to-day reality involved solitary work in an office by myself. I missed the long, mundane logistics meetings at my former church, when I could look across the table at my friends, who were trying to stay awake. I missed seeing my colleagues five times a day for no reason other than getting paper clips from the supply room. I missed the way we talked idealistically about how we would do things if we were the boss.

I missed my friends.

Even though I knew something was amiss, I wasn't willing to admit it yet. Really, I wasn't willing to allow myself places and people of refuge. I thought that because the church was young and fragile, I couldn't allow myself to have fun or relax with friends. I felt I had to be consumed by my work, in heart and mind, if anything was going to come of it. What I didn't realize was that if I pushed this hard, the church might survive, but I might not survive with it.

Loneliness doesn't necessarily mean being alone. Loneliness is the lack of peace inside when you feel like you're going it alone, when it seems like no one else is in this with you. You can feel lonely by yourself, in a crowd, even with your family and friends. We feel lonely when our actual relational intimacy doesn't match our desired relational intimacy.

The former surgeon general of the United States wrote in the *Harvard Business Review*, "Loneliness and weak social connections are associated with a reduction in lifespan similar to that caused by smoking fifteen cigarettes a day and even greater than that associated with obesity."[1] The article explains that our bodies become more aware of threats while lonely. The stress releases increased hormones that cause physical changes in our bodies.

Would my anxiety and heart pains decrease if I laughed with my friends? I wondered.

I finally admitted to Kristy that I was lonely, but I was pretty sure my friends in Atlanta had moved on. After all, they were successful in their careers and had active social lives in different parts of the city.

Who has time for old friendships?

So I fought the feelings of loneliness by doubling down on work. I told myself that if I could just get to a certain point of fulfillment and stability, I would allow myself time for friendships again.

As I watched Scotty's example of investing in friendships, however, I began to see the rich treasure that was lacking in my own life. I still had an inclination toward self-protection and plenty of excuses about being too busy for friends, but I admired Scotty's willingness to take the risk of loving, being loved, and engaging in true friendship.

While we talked about loneliness, Scotty told me about the "porcupine's dilemma"—a metaphor used by philosophers to explain the challenges of human intimacy. The German philosopher Arthur Schopenhauer described it this way: "A number of porcupines huddled together for warmth on a cold day in winter; but, as they began to prick one another with their quills, they were obliged to disperse. However, the cold drove them together again, when just the same thing happened. At last, after many turns of huddling and dispersing, they discovered that they would be best off by remaining at a little distance from one another."[2]

As imperfect people, we are both driven to and repelled by doing life together. So we choose a casual relational state rather than an intimate one, thus ensuring only moderate satisfaction in having our relational needs met.

I may not be warm, but at least I'm not being pricked, we think.

This thought feeds our fear of rejection, isolation, and loneliness. It was time for me to figure out how to be a relational porcupine. Yes, I was risking injury. But I was ready to come out of the cold.

A Pain-Free Heart

DEBBIE WAS SCOTTY'S GIRLFRIEND in high school. It was a teen romance, a step above puppy love. Their dating life had zero drama, lots of kissing, and great dancing. Scotty and Debbie would shag dance, combining the old jitterbug with the slower rhythms of Motown. She was the only person he trusted with his heart throughout high school.

In the fall of 1968, when Scotty was a freshman at UNC, he received a phone call early in the morning. Debbie had been killed in a car wreck.

Another car wreck. Another death.

The numbness that had crept in at his mom's death took over. Scotty made lame excuses for why he couldn't be a pallbearer at her funeral. If his mom's death prompted him to bury his heart in a pain-free lockbox, Debbie's death gave him another ten locks to put on the latch. Without making a conscious decision, he determined to never allow himself to risk feeling relational pain again. He set up an idol of a pain-free heart.

Four years later, when he married Darlene, the idol was still in tow.

It made sense to me. Perhaps our desire for painlessness is prompted by a memory of Eden. The problem is that there are no shortcuts to get there.

We all seek connection somewhere—to someone or something—because that's the way we're wired. But when we encounter a porcupine, we think we won't be able to sustain the next round of pain, so we decide not to move toward vulnerability. Still, we can't suppress the longing for what vulnerability alone gives us: connection and belonging.

The apostle Paul wrote counterintuitively about pain and weakness in his letter to the Corinthian church:

Three times I pleaded with the Lord about [my thorn], that it should leave me. But he said to me, "My grace is sufficient for you, for my power is made perfect in weakness." Therefore I will boast all the more gladly of my weaknesses, so that the power of Christ may rest upon me. For the sake of Christ, then, I am content with weaknesses, insults, hardships, persecutions, and calamities. For when I am weak, then I am strong.

2 CORINTHIANS 12:8-10

Paul said he would boast in weakness, not because he loved the weakness but because God moves into the weakness. God's compassionate presence in Paul's suffering confirmed his standing as the beloved. And that suffering—the fact that Paul couldn't remedy it himself—meant he had to rely wholly and completely on God. When Paul was at his weakest, when he was unable to do anything about his situation, the Almighty became his strength.

Likewise, it's in our vulnerability with God and with others that we see how deeply we are loved. It gives others the opportunity to stand with us and prop us up in our struggles. This is the gift and risk of both loving and being loved.

C. S. Lewis writes,

> To love at all is to be vulnerable. Love anything and your heart will be wrung and possibly broken. If you want to make sure of keeping it intact you must give it to no one, not even an animal. Wrap it carefully round with hobbies and little luxuries; avoid all entanglements. Lock it up safe in the casket or coffin of your selfishness. But in that casket, safe, dark, motionless, airless, it will change. It will not be broken; it will become unbreakable, impenetrable, irredeemable. To love is to be vulnerable.[3]

"I carry scars and marks of my pain, and that's okay," Scotty told me when we were talking about his losses. "The goal of the Christian life isn't to get over stuff but to grow through it. Jesus' promise of an abundant life doesn't just include an abundance of things we enjoy but also an abundance of things that will make us more like him. Christlikeness and greater intimacy with Jesus are sabotaged when we make a goal of having a pain-free life and heart."

"Honestly, it sounds exhausting to open myself up to pain," I said.

"You know, as I've become healthier, my laugh is quicker and louder, and my tears are saltier and more frequent. There's something about vulnerability that makes us more alive. We become more grace-aware and self-aware, and therefore more others-aware."

My definition of bravery has changed in the last few years. I used to think it involved climbing mountains and making business deals, but I think those things can just as easily be motivated by fear as by bravery.

True courage means gazing into our pain through the lens of our belovedness.

For me, it meant beginning to open my inner thoughts and emotions to my wife, pursuing my friends with more intentionality, and wholeheartedly giving and receiving the warmth of friendship. Even with the pain that comes with it.

The Gift of Vulnerability

SCOTTY BEGAN ABUSING ALCOHOL in high school as a reaction to negative feelings inside himself, namely loneliness and shame. The altered state brought about through substance abuse gave the illusion of strength. As a seventeen-year-old kid traveling with the band and playing at fraternity parties, he drank to enjoy the night but also to survive the night. He wanted to feel invincible.

Notice me, but don't know me, he was silently pleading.

"When I was buzzed, I wasn't afraid to look anybody in the eye or be seen," Scotty told me. "Things that scared me no longer scared me."

"So what exactly did substance abuse give you?" I asked.

"We want drugs and alcohol to do two things for us: numb the pain and give the illusion of 'okayness.' When I was a little older than you are now, God began to say to me, through his Word and through good friends, 'You're not as free as I intend.' Part of coming out from behind the curtain was taking the risk of being seen and known in relationships."

"What did that look like?" I asked.

"I came to vulnerability begrudgingly," Scotty said. "I saw it before I wanted it for myself. My mentor, Jack Miller, was a very vulnerable, free man. He intrigued me. I was drawn to him, but I was skilled at propping up my inner world. I was competent at being transparent but not really vulnerable. I simply wasn't willing to feel deeply the loss, pain, and shame of my story. Through the 'gift' of burnout, God began the process of healing me and freeing me."

Brené Brown, bestselling author and research professor at the University of Houston, studied people who had a strong sense of love and belonging.

What did these people have in common?

What did they know and practice?

What Brown discovered, to her surprise, was that these people have the courage to be imperfect, the courage to be kind to themselves and others. Their connections are birthed out of authenticity.

Brown writes in her book *Daring Greatly*, "Vulnerability is the birthplace of love, belonging, joy, courage, empathy, and creativity. It is the source of hope, empathy, accountability, and authenticity. If we want greater clarity in our purpose or deeper and more meaningful spiritual lives, vulnerability is the path."[4]

I believe her research revealed what has always been human—and what Jesus taught from the beginning of his ministry: "Blessed are the poor in spirit, for theirs is the kingdom of heaven" (Matthew 5:3). I like how pastor and author Eugene Peterson words this verse in *The Message*: "You're blessed when you're at the end of your rope. With less of you there is more of God and his rule."

Our way forward into love and belonging is as rewarding as heaven but as scary as hell. If we want to be less lonely, we need to be more known, and that means letting people into our weaknesses rather than constantly covering them. We will continue poking others and getting poked, but ultimately this vulnerability brings us the warmth we desire.

I asked Scotty for his definition of vulnerability.

"Vulnerability is the willingness to feel—to sit in the reality of your story," he said. "It's not just acknowledging the data of your story but becoming more honest and at home before God. When we do, we become emotionally self-aware and more present with others."

"So not just the data, but the implication of the data?" I asked. "Embracing the feeling?"

"Yes, we have to slow down enough to sit in the implications of our stories. The beauty and brokenness, the wounds and worries, the messiness and lack of control."

◎   ◎   ◎

Years ago, at a dinner with friends, one of my best friends said in passing, "Rusty plays his cards real close."

A few people laughed, and the conversation moved on seamlessly. He didn't mean it in a hostile way, and I wasn't embarrassed. But I was curious.

"Kristy, do you think I play my cards close to my chest?" I asked once we were in the car.

"Yes."

"What does that mean?" I asked.

"You don't even tell me some things. You know what that means."

"What do I do?" I asked.

"You welcome people, but you don't really let them in. You bring them close, but not too close. You're more open to me now than you used to be, but you're still protective around most people."

She was right. Just the thought of being vulnerable sends shivers through me. It's easier for me to type something vulnerable on a computer, even if it will be read by thousands of people at some later date, than to stand face-to-face and be vulnerable with someone.

"My porcupine dilemma kicks in quickly," I said to Scotty. "I want connection so I move closer, and then I get poked and I back up. Or I fear I will get poked even if there's no threat."

"I've been hurt enough. Rejected enough. I'm not going to risk that again," Scotty said, summarizing my thoughts. "Russ, healthy, self-aware people know their beauty and their brokenness. They are continually growing in their awareness of how they impact others and how others impact them."

Perhaps we learn the most about vulnerability from God himself, who insists on coming after us. He sent his Son to leave his heavenly throne and become a human being. He humbled himself so he could reveal himself to us. Who would have thought that God's office would be at the bottom of the ladder, not the top?

Before we know God, we are known by God. This truth brings rest to my relentless effort to know God "enough."

Toward the end of the letter to the Galatians, Paul writes of the effects of the gospel: believers move progressively (though imperfectly) toward righteousness, love, and wholeness. What resonates with me is the phrase Paul used to motivate the church: "Now that you have come to know God, or rather to be known by God" (Galatians 4:9). I learned that the word *rather* probably means something more like "more importantly."

Seminary professor and author J. I. Packer writes,

> What matters supremely, therefore, is not, in the last analysis, the fact that I know God, but the larger fact which underlies it—the fact that he knows me. . . . There is tremendous relief in knowing that his love to me is utterly realistic, based at every point on prior knowledge of the worst about me, so that no discovery now can disillusion him about me, in the way that I am so often disillusioned about myself. . . . He wants me as His friend, and desires to be my friend, and has given His son to die for me in order to realise this purpose.[5]

God doesn't welcome us because he has to—because we prayed a prayer, became moral, or got religious. God welcomes us because he takes pleasure in us. God is saying,

> *I know that son of mine.*
> *I know that daughter.*
> *They're a real mess sometimes.*
> *I know all about them, and I love them.*

This is the thought that soothes my soul and frees me. It empowers me to face pain and walk into relationships, knowing the risk. If I really believe this, it will affect everything: my marriage, my parenting, my friendships.

●   ●   ●

From Scotty
I Was Forty-Five

It was July of 1995. I was sitting on Dan Allender's back porch in Colorado, soaking in the deep blue sky and the 12-percent-humidity awesomeness of Colorado air. I noticed something rimming the back of his property.

"So, Dan, what's with the razor wire fence back there? You must be trying to keep some *big* bears out."

"Heck no, those guys are keeping *us* out. Those are the feds. That property holds big-boy missiles positioned in underground silos. If China or Russia were to get a bit testy, the US could attack and launch nuclear warheads faster than you can cross your legs. The bears don't have a chance," Dan said.

This term "nuclear warhead" was about to become a gospel metaphor for me, with my heart as the strike zone.

Darlene had been processing her story of sexual abuse and her family of origin issues with Dan for six years. The healthier she became, the more it disrupted the equilibrium of our marriage. As a pastor, I've seen this scenario play out many times. Couples get stuck—and quite comfortable—in unhealthy relational patterns. Then, through the work of God's Spirit, one of the spouses owns their brokenness, seeks help, and moves into a season of growth and freedom. Quite naturally, that spouse (Darlene, in our case) begins to want more and better for their mate and their marriage.

It was one thing to help other couples, but now it was my turn to be pastored. I was right in the middle of disruption-city as I sat on Dan's deck, and it wasn't a comfortable chair. Darlene's growing health and emotional bandwidth both confused and threatened me. As she grieved her abuse and tasted new freedom, Darlene wept more tears, got angrier, and laughed louder than ever before. At first I thought she was less "spiritual" as she began to walk in freedom rather than legalistic striving.

I was hoping Dan would coddle me in my confusion and coach me into patience until Darlene got over "this," whatever *this* was. Instead, he got face to face with me—almost too close—and spoke words that became a freedom tattoo on my heart, "Scotty, as long as your cry for relief is louder than your cry for a changed heart, you're never going to grow as a man."

I wanted a hug; instead, one of heaven's silos opened up and Dan delivered a grace warhead to the idols and insecurities of my heart. Direct hit. I'd never felt more exposed, more known, and more loved.

Grace in Marriage

SCOTTY GREW UP A TAR HEEL, just twenty miles from the University of North Carolina campus, so it was natural for him to attend school there. He began in the Pharmacy School but ended up as a religion major. In 1970, during his junior year, Scotty met Darlene at a church meeting in a house outside of Burlington, North Carolina. She was studying fashion design in Atlanta after having partied her way out of East Carolina University.

Darlene was ten days into her Christian faith journey, drop-dead gorgeous, and enamored with Jesus' love for her. Scotty and Darlene began dating while living in different cities. They wrote letters to each other and saw each other on school breaks when they returned home to Burlington.

After they dated for eighteen months, Scotty asked Darlene to marry him while they were driving in a car. As a testament to his fear and avoidance of pain, he requested that she not respond right away but pray about it for a week first.

They were married on May 5, 1972, the semester before Scotty graduated from UNC. They moved to Philadelphia so Scotty could attend Westminster Seminary, where his theological knowledge continued to grow, though his heart wasn't yet ready for the gospel's implications.

As I reflected on the challenges that come with working and raising a family, and the implications of the gospel for my life, I thought about the marriage between the first man and woman before the Fall. Each of them chose a communal reality over a private, self-oriented one. For me, the transition into this union has been harder than I expected. Marriage doesn't cause selfishness or arrogance; it exposes what's always been there. And marriage doesn't magically heal the emotional trauma from the past; it exposes it and gives us, God willing, a place to become vulnerable with it.

I thought I came into marriage as a young man with ambition and adventure in his heart, but underneath was the reservoir of pain I wasn't even aware of. I desperately needed to process the wounds from my childhood and the rejection I felt.

"What do you make of the imagery of 'leaving and cleaving' in Genesis?" I asked Scotty while we talked about vulnerability.

"I think the ultimate application of leaving, cleaving, and weaving is with our true bridegroom, Jesus. In other words, the more the gospel permeates my heart, the more I'll inhabit my relationships in a healthy way. With Darlene, who I've been married to for forty-eight years now, it was always easier for me to leave my past than to cleave and weave with her. Physical intimacy was a lot easier for me than emotional intimacy."

"You were ready to leave your past and your childhood family?" I asked.

"Oh yes, big time. My mom left me when I was eleven years old, and my dad never . . ."

"But did you really leave?" I interrupted him and immediately wished I hadn't.

"No, of course not. My attempt to 'leave' my mom was a fruitless effort to deny the searing pain of my loss. I didn't have a single picture of Mom up anywhere in our house. When you work hard to build a pain-free life, you never succeed. The pain will get repackaged and show up in other ways. Darlene and I both were ready to get out of our homes of origin, but we brought a lot of extra baggage from our families with us. We all do. It took years, and a lot of God's grace, to recognize our anger, sadness, and triggers."

"So what helped you guys change that pattern?" I asked.

"Jesus came to heal broken hearts and set captives free. I needed to see how I've been both a victim and an agent of sin—both harmed and foolish. That's when God's grace becomes necessary, real, and precious. God resists the proud but gives grace to the humble. And I needed to be humbled."

I thought about the prerequisite of humility for vulnerability and my preferred modes of competency and distance.

"We enter our spouse's weakness and brokenness to the extent that we enter our own," Scotty continued. "And we can only extend the grace we have received from our loving Father. I needed to own how I contributed to the dysfunction and lack of health in our marriage. My silent self-righteousness was lethal in our relationship. I wanted her to be 'up' because I feared being sad and melancholic. *Would you please just not be so sad?* was often the silent message I was sending her."

"What else made marriage difficult for you?" I asked.

"We project our need for control onto others—especially the parts of our story that we haven't processed. As we've talked about, I grew up with body image and food control issues. I was overweight, and then I became a radical exerciser. But I never entered any of that pain, so I projected it onto Darlene. I assumed she would wear a size four dress forever. If she reaches for a second or third cookie, I find myself wanting to control that."

"What do you think is at the core of that problem?" I asked.

"I was unwilling to deal with my shame and engage Darlene's heart. I could be sexually intimate with her with no problem, but I felt incompetent to enter the messy parts of her story and her longings. I kept propping up my way of life: *Let's just get through these first few years of church planting. Let's get the kids out of diapers. Let's get the kids self-sufficient.* I always found a way to rationalize why there was no time (or even need) for vulnerability so I could preserve my idol of a pain-free heart. Darlene was, and is, an amazing, beautiful woman who loves Jesus more than I do and wasn't afraid of anything. It seemed like she could handle herself and I could handle myself, so I thought I was off the hook from the messiness of love. Darlene's decision to seek wholeness was the greatest gift to our marriage. It cracked me open."

Scotty paused, as if he were flashing back over the past few decades. "You know, pain isn't a bad thing. It's just something that needs to be stewarded. If I want to have a garden, I've got to do some tilling. That's where vulnerability starts, specifically when it comes to dealing with our pain and brokenness. At first, you're tilling up roots and stones."

◉   ◉   ◉

When Kristy and I had our first daughter, we brought her home to our little two-bedroom house in Grant Park, Atlanta. For the previous two years, we'd renovated that shoebox house, filling it with love and a bounding golden retriever named Thomas, preparing to bring a baby into our family.

After we arrived home from the hospital, I helped Kristy and our baby girl get settled. Five minutes later, I was working on my next project—painting our little office in the middle of the house. I was loud, and the paint smell filled the little bungalow. Kristy politely complained to me, so I opened the door and ran a fan.

Kristy was up and down all day and all night, feeding our little girl. I helped every once and a while, but for the most part I kept to myself. Kristy and I were roommates living side by side rather than face to face marital partners on a journey.

"What is this marriage?" she asked me one night, crying in the kitchen. The paint smell still hung in the air.

"This is our marriage," I said.

"Do we just live together, or is there more?"

It would have been easy to dismiss this conversation, to chalk it up to a lack of sleep or changes in her hormones. But I knew this was about something deeper. The question revealed my mistake, which I'd been making from day one of our marriage. I treated her as a best friend to live around but not a wife and partner to share my heart and life with.

Kristy wasn't questioning our marriage; she was commenting on the state of our marriage. She was tired, having endured a brutal labor and an eventual C-section and the responsibilities of caring for a newborn. My lack of empathy and gentleness compounded her weary state.

"I'm sorry," I said. "I did all of this wrong."

"We have to be in this together. I need you in this with me."

It was a turning point in our marriage—one of many. It was a chance for me to grow in the grace of God. This was the beginning of our marriage transitioning from independence to unity. We had two more daughters in the following four years, and with the birth of each little girl, the Holy Spirit birthed in me an increase of gentleness. God is still using those girls to soften my heart to them, and to Kristy, and subsequently he is patiently transforming my rough heart toward smoother edges.

It's slow and imperfect, but it's a start.

In our belovedness, both beautiful and broken, we are free to be our imperfect selves in our relationships. Knowing our identity is secure, we no longer have to entangle each other with impossible demands. I see now how resisting vulnerability ends up sabotaging intimacy with Kristy. And in my resistance, I tend to transfer the sadness or anger or frustration from my pain onto her.

I'm learning that health in marriage (or any close relationship, for that matter) isn't perfection but each person saying, "I know I need God's grace, so I'm comfortable with your need for God's grace too."

●   ●   ●

From Scotty

I Was Fifty

It was October of 2000. The domino effect of grace was at work in my life—felling my fears, excuses, and heart idols. Now God had my next assignment: connecting at a heart level with my daughter, Kristin.

Fishing is the common language my son, Scott, and I enjoy, so it has always been easy for me to be with him in a relaxed and present way. Our relationship was forged beside small ponds, a neighborhood river, and the shoreline of Destin, Florida. We learned to fly-fish together at Rocky Mountain National Park in Colorado and went on fly-in excursions to glacier lakes in Canada and trips to Alaska to fish for salmon.

But with Kristin, it was different. From the day Mom was ripped from my life, I've been awkward, imbalanced, and insecure around women and girls. I knew how to love Kristin when she was a little girl, and I'm thankful for fun memories documented by troves of pictures. But as she got older, our relationship got more complicated, and I retreated from her.

I wish my story hadn't run through the valley of death. I wish I'd had a mother during those awkward middle school years. I wish I had sisters. I wish fear hadn't taken hold in my heart so deeply and so early. I wanted much more for my kids than I received—and more than I gave.

Thankfully, the gospel is a story of redemption, not do-overs—a story of all things becoming new, not old things paralyzing us with guilt. It's a journey of owning our stories without making excuses. The way of grace is a healing path, breaking the power of shame and offering the hope of resurrection. It was time for me to move toward Kristin—to "risk or rust," as my spiritual dad, Jack Miller, was fond of saying.

"Kristin, it's Dad," I said over the phone. "Can we get together soon?"

She was in her early twenties, and I was early into a peace I'd never felt before. My goal for getting together with her wasn't to promote a newer version of myself, to make promises I couldn't keep, or even to ask for forgiveness. It was to listen. I wanted to hear Kristin's heart, fully realizing she probably had some painful things to say to me.

We met over a cup of coffee at a café.

"Kristin, thanks for meeting me here. As you know, your mom and I have been doing a lot of work, individually and in our relationship. It's made me think about us—you and me. I'm here because I want something different for us. I realize I haven't been very emotionally present in your life—or anybody else's, including your mom's. It pains me to say it, but it's true."

I paused to catch my breath and let her respond.

"Thanks, Dad. I'm glad you and Mom are working on your stuff. As for us—"

"Here's my question, Kristin," I interrupted. Maybe I was too anxious to finish my intro, or maybe I was a bit nervous about what she would say. "What do you remember about me as your dad? What memories stand out? I'm not looking for kudos. What do I need to hear?"

She couldn't have anticipated my question, but she didn't pause with her answer. It's as though she'd been waiting for this moment.

"I must have been about eleven or twelve. I could tell I was becoming too much for you, and I watched you disappear into more ministry." She didn't say it with anger, but neither did she hurry on to thank me for braces, a car, and college.

It wasn't easy to hear. It hurt, but it was a good hurt. This was the path of vulnerability.

"Thank you," I said. "I want to know more about what that felt like and how it impacted you."

If I had tried to hurry up an apology, it would have sabotaged the moment and derailed any movement forward. That meeting at the café was almost twenty years ago. We continue to talk, heal, and hope.

Grace in Parenting

THE FIRST TIME I MET SCOTTY back in that barn, he told the story about apologizing to his daughter for not being as present and nurturing as he could have been. When I heard him share that story with the larger group, I knew I had to chase him down to mentor me. *What fuels a grown man to reopen the past with his grown children?* I wondered.

Scotty's daughter was strong willed and his son was compliant, so they responded to their parents' shortcomings in different ways. But they both experienced pain as a result of Scotty's failure to parent their hearts as they grew up. This omission wasn't conscious, but it was culpable. As Darlene and Scotty moved into greater vulnerability, their kids reacted compassionately to them, knowing they'd tried to parent well. There was sadness in the story line, but that became where they were able to heal together.

This had me thinking, *If vulnerability depends on being seen, who sees us more clearly than our children?*

They see us when the mask is off, when the true self emerges from behind the presented self that we show to the world. My daughters know this gap between my presented self and my true self, and I have to step into that space to live in honesty and confession with them. Scotty modeled confession for Kristy and me, so when we became aware of our screwups with our children, we began to sit our children down or lie beside them in bed and confess our mistakes to them.

Spiritual writer Anne Lamott reflected on this practice for Salon's annual Trust Me on This series, in which famous people share life lessons. Regarding confession as a way to connect with her child, she writes, "A tradition of that is something I've been able to pass on to my son. He's grown up with a mother who's willing to be contrite, to get to the bottom of things—and to see that sometimes it's me who I've been mad at. The tradition of letting your children watch you ask for forgiveness is beautiful."

Usually my parental mistakes, and my apologies, come in the evening when I'm tired from the day and wish my girls would simply comply with my every direction as speedily as the Road Runner.

"Grab your things, put away your jackets and shoes, and head to the shower," I dictated one night as I parked the car in the garage. It was a school night, and we'd just returned from a quick bite to eat.

Two of the girls showed up in the house and made their way to the bathroom. My eight-year-old showed up five minutes later, frustrated, with her jacket and one shoe.

"I can't find my other shoe," she said.

"What do you mean, you can't find your shoe?" I barked.

"It's not there."

"Didn't you just have them on in the restaurant and when you walked to the car?"

"Yeah, but it is gone," she said. "It's not in the car."

I marched her back to the garage and watched her search the car again. I had her search all around the car, under the car, and in the driveway. Then I searched.

The shoe was gone.

"You have to keep up with your stuff," I lectured, my intensity growing. "You never keep up with your stuff. Mom and I bought those shoes with our money that we earned by working hard, and you don't appreciate any of it."

I continued to rail on her about the mysterious missing shoe until we were back in the house. I'm not a yeller, but I have a level of intensity that can shame and crush the soul of a person, even my child. Especially my child.

My daughter took her shower, put on her pajamas, and crawled into her bed crying. As I stopped and caught my breath from my provider-dad lecture, the Holy Spirit helped me see my impatience. I crawled into her bunk bed.

"Babe, I need to apologize. I was upset you lost your shoe. I was tired, but I was wrong. I'm asking God to help me with my impatience. I need God to help me in that area, and I want to do better. I'm sorry. I love you very much."

There are millions of "shoe moments" in raising kids—those times we tip over the top, not because of the shoe but because of a million earlier moments. In most cases, the shoe shows up eventually, as it did in our case a month later, wedged precariously between two seats. The shoe's reappearance resulted in a family celebration and laughter because my girls remembered how absurdly upset I'd been when it went missing.

To my continued surprise, the vulnerability that comes with confession only increases my relationship with my daughters and welcomes them to admit their own mistakes.

Many of us give lip service to the idea that our children belong to God, but in practice, we rely on them to define us or to set our mood. This reality reveals that we don't just love them but are actually using them to justify our own existence. When I find myself in this kind of selfish, vampire-like parenting, I know I'm sucking love from them instead of reflecting God's love to them. This puts undue pressure on our children to validate us, and it reflects our lack of belief that we are already worthy because of the gospel.

"What enables us to parent to our child's heart, even while they are behaving in ways that appall or embarrass us, is our belovedness," Scotty says.

That is, after all, the way our heavenly Father parents us.

Connection in Friendship

KRISTY AND I WOULD SEE our old friends from Atlanta a couple of times a year at parties, but months would pass without connecting. This pattern became routine: catching up at parties, dispersing around Atlanta, and then waiting to catch up again six months later.

"We've had a hard time making friends," my friend Chris said. We had just shared a meal together at a Christmas party, and all the friends I'd been missing were there. The vulnerability of Chris's comment was admirable and inspiring. I felt the same way, but I didn't have the courage to speak my loneliness to anyone besides Kristy.

After Chris spoke, similar echoes resounded around the table. We all missed each other, but we thought everyone else had moved on. In reality, we all had loneliness in our veins even as our bodies were busy. We were leading churches, running businesses, and participating in our communities, but we were lonely.

That moment marked a turning point for our little group. We

decided to meet for long dinners in restaurants around the city every four to six weeks, without our children, so we could talk without distraction. After we'd been sharing dinners together for six months, we decided that wasn't enough, so we began taking trips together, extending our time and deepening our connection.

Scotty regularly asks me, "How are the boys?" or "How is the gospel posse?" I think this is his way of making sure I'm still in relationship with these friends and not isolating myself again. Sure, we're all busy, but we're too busy *not* to move toward one another in gospel love.

Two of my best friends, Drew and Seth, started a church a few years before I did. After Kristy and I started our church, we found ourselves unsure how to navigate being people's friends but also their pastor, and I found myself talking to Drew and Seth more and more.

"So there was this party, and we didn't get invited," I said. The three of us were gathered around a table at a local bagel shop.

"Well, you know the two saddest words in the human language?" Drew said. He answered himself: "What party?"

We all laughed.

"Did it hurt your and Kristy's feelings?" Seth asked.

"I think we're processing it. It's a bit of a head-scratcher. We're not entitled to be invited to every party. We understand that's not reality. But yeah, we were sad. It didn't make sense."

"It's okay to be sad about that," Drew said. "And it's okay for them to *not* invite you. You're their friend but also their pastor."

"As pastors, we are spiritual fathers, in a way," Seth added, "and sometimes you just don't want your dad at your party."

I left the conversation feeling heard and relieved. It was good to have safe friends who listened and cared, who made me feel like I belonged.

"All-season friends are your safe friends, your inner circle," Scotty told me. "They're the people who will be around when you feel betrayed or rejected or depressed. Time plus grace plus tears plus fun equals friendship. We have to be willing to let people enter the season we're in and to enter the season they're in. That was part of my growth in vulnerability: to invite my friends into my pain for the first time. To let Michael and Scott weep over me as I admitted I'd never been to my mom's grave. And then to let Dan weep with me when I first voiced my story of sexual abuse."

"How did you know you could trust them?" I asked.

"Trust is built in a friendship over time as you let yourself be known. Think of your relationships as circles of intimacy, with a small circle in the center and larger circles going outward. The bull's-eye for each of us is God—only he knows us fully and loves us fully. We won't learn to be intimate with anyone else without that safety."

With my all-season friends, I have only one motive, and that's to be and have a good friend. It's taken time, but I've come to believe that these guys don't really care if I'm a huge success in this world. They just want to know and love me.

Sometimes I still hear the fearful voice inside me that says, *They don't want to hear that. They're too busy for that.*

If I keep that voice in check, and by God's grace sometimes I do, then I come back around to an important question: *Would I want them to share that with me?*

The answer is usually yes, and when I share with them, the response is usually loving-kindness.

In *The Gifts of Imperfection*, Brené Brown writes, "We cultivate love when we allow our most vulnerable and powerful selves to be deeply seen and known, and when we honor the spiritual connection that grows from that offering with trust, respect, kindness and affection."[7] I see Brown's findings as embedded within gospel truth: in our weakness, we are made strong. God uses vulnerability to spur us to gentle, if imperfect, regard for those around us. Vulnerability helps us to be less judgmental and prepares us to repent when necessary—without deflection, transference, or projection.

We are all wearing fig leaves of some kind, waiting for someone else to recognize us and show us love.

From Scotty
Prayerful Contemplation

1. What do you think is the difference between transparency and vulnerability? Describe both the freedom and the threat of vulnerability you have experienced.

2. Who in your life demonstrates humility, vulnerability, and authenticity to you?

3. Consider asking the following questions to those you walk the closest with (for example, a spouse, a parent, a friend, a child). Context will determine which of these questions to ask.

   - What are you most inclined to pray for me?
   - What encourages you the most about my heart and life?
   - What would a healthier and freer me look like?
   - What seems to define me more than the love of God and the riches of the gospel?
   - What would it look like to love you well in this season?
   - How can I best pursue and attend to your heart?

AN UNHURRIED, NON-ANXIOUS SPIRIT IS TRUE SUCCESS.

The Busy Heart

SCOTTY AND I WERE SITTING in a booth at a sushi restaurant near his home in Franklin. I was coming off a Monday filled with work, overloading the day with sermon preparation, staff meetings, and email replies so I could drive to Nashville in the evening and be with Scotty all day Tuesday. Spending time with Scotty was restful and refreshing, but my heart was busy from a weekend of family and ministry, and a Monday filled with two days' worth of work plus a four-hour drive.

"Did you feel busy for all those years with work and family?" I asked him.

"Well, life can quickly become a series of events," he replied. "I always think about it as a busy heart before a busy schedule. If the gospel is not the greater narrative of our lives, we subtly begin to feel the need for something to make us whole, to validate us. That pressure will create an anxious and busy heart."

"I get that. My heart is busy so often—sort of itchy," I said. "I itch to look at my phone rather than just exist or be or breathe.

It always feels easier to find the next thing to check or watch or consume. In a way, all the hurry makes me feel important."

Scotty nodded. "We are made to be productive. When God said to his first son and daughter, 'Fill the earth with my glory,' that's an awesome, life-fulfilling calling—one we still have. Be creative. Build culture. Make beauty. The trouble comes when we believe Christianity is more about doing things *for* Jesus than doing all things *with* Jesus. Sadly, my busyness became most pronounced after I became a Christian. Though I really believed we only enter heaven by God's grace, my introduction to 'discipleship' led me to believe we can put a bigger smile on God's face by doing more and trying harder."

"What helped your busy heart?" I asked, aching to know what could help my own.

"I became intrigued by the peaceful, shame-free life Adam and Eve enjoyed in Eden—and the life that's promised us in the new creation to come. Even now, God calls us to linger longer, to Sabbath more, so we can be set free from anxiety in his presence. 'Be still and know that I am God' is an offer he makes to us for consistent, calm state of being."

Scotty's words reminded me of something an old boss had told me. Todd started and led a church in Tampa for eighteen years before moving to Atlanta. I loved reporting to Todd. He was twenty-five years ahead of me in age, wisdom, and craft, and he cared for people above bureaucracy. A year after starting our church, Todd invited me to lunch, and we met at Chick-fil-A. After catching up for a while, he pulled out an index card from his front left pocket. On it were written three things, numbered.

I don't remember the first two, but I clearly remember the final one.

"And the last thing," he said. "When I started and pastored our church, I only felt free when I left town. It was as if seeing the Welcome to Town sign in the rearview mirror signaled my heart to let go. Russ, I don't have any pointers on how to be free while you're in your town working, but I know you have to figure it out."

He was describing my pattern of life precisely: feeling busy with work, being unsure when work stopped, and consequently being plagued by a frazzled heart and a frantic mind. I was encouraged by his words to leave town to refuel, but he also helped me see that I needed to form a life that was sustainably thriving day to day.

His advice was timely, since by this point I'd experienced my heart palpitations, and then I began waking up aching and sore, as if I'd survived a car wreck the previous day. I was at my personal maximum capacity, and every additional ounce of weight had me crumpling. This weight disappeared only when I boarded an airplane or when we drove south to the beach. I would enjoy stillness for a few days, but then I'd return home to the same cycle.

When I was in the thick of launching our church, Kristy, the girls, and I drove to a neighboring suburb for a gathering with Kristy's family. When I hugged my younger sister-in-law, I said, "I feel like I haven't seen you in forever."

She said, sort of playfully, "I've been here. You don't come to family events anymore."

I laughed and guided the conversation elsewhere, but I couldn't shake her comment. She pointed out what perhaps many people were seeing. I wasn't showing up for a lot of life because part of my life felt overwhelming. There was always a reason to stay back, to work on something, or to isolate myself, thinking it would help me to catch my breath. My busy heart was keeping me busy but never free.

The book *Margin* by Richard Swenson describes my life at this time well.

> We must have some room to breathe. We need freedom to think and permission to heal. Our relationships are being starved to death by velocity. No one has the time to listen, let alone love. Our children lay wounded on the ground, run over by our high-speed good intentions. Is God now pro-exhaustion? Doesn't He lead people beside the still waters anymore? Who plundered those wide-open spaces of the past, and how can we get them back? There are no fallow lands for our emotions to lie down and rest in.[1]

In other words, our work can progress while we suffer. We may see busyness for God as a badge of honor, but a busy heart is usually a futile attempt at medicating pain, filling a void, or dealing with failure.

In the sushi restaurant, when Scotty talked to me about a busy heart, I could feel myself wanting to graph my emotions. If I could draw a perfect flowchart of fear and anxiety and stress, maybe I could understand them, and then I wouldn't be as prone to fall victim to them. Maybe then I could be free, not just at the beach or in the mountains, but also in our hometown, where my life has daily demands.

"I don't know about graphing stress and anxiety, Russ," Scotty said. "But we can certainly ask which comes first: the stress or the anxiety. I think there's an interplay. People often use these words interchangeably, but they're not exactly the same. Fear isn't a bad emotion; it's a reality to be honored and understood. Someone who experiences fear doesn't necessarily have an anxiety disorder. And some stressed people aren't afraid; they're just driven—living more by performance-based acceptance than by God's radical acceptance of us in Jesus."

The truth is, we fear what growing still would mean.

What might we hear?

What might arise from below the surface?

But if we never get off the merry-go-round of busyness, we miss all the life and transformation that is there waiting for us.

○　　○　　○

From Scotty

My Mom

I will never forget one morning when I was six or seven years old, before Mom left for Greensboro to manage Scotty's Children's Shop. She placed her hands on the sides of my head, looked me in the eyes, and with a huge smile said, "I'm going to bring you home a pair of red clamdiggers today." I wasn't an elementary-school fashionista, and I wasn't thrilled over the prospect of sporting clamdiggers, the embarrassing three-quarter-length pants with a white racing stripe down the side. But Mom could have said anything. She could have said she was going to bring me a kite, a turtle, some marbles, or a bag of M&M'S. It would have had the same impact. She was bringing me a gift, and it thrilled my heart.

With her beautiful brunette hair, dark brown eyes, and abounding love, that lady lit up rooms everywhere she went. I never saw her flustered, and only once did I see her in tears. She loved loud and she loved large—and she loved me. Of course, those clamdiggers weren't going to be light blue or pale yellow; they were going to be red, *bright* red. I felt her passion, her joy in doing something for me, and I relished the certainty of her coming home at the end of the day to keep loving me.

In the evenings, our routine suppers consisted of chipped beef mixed with a can of mushroom soup and served over a piece of toast, canned Green Giant peas, and instant mashed potatoes with a dollop of butter on top. One evening after supper, Mom got up from the table, opened the cabinet above the refrigerator, and lifted out the ugliest cake I'd ever seen. My dad, my brother, and I had not given any hints about wanting cake, but somehow Mom decided her boys needed a cake. And there it was, in the middle of the table, barely recognizable. The three-layer cake was topped with icing so thick and rich that the cake pulled apart in multiple chunks of baked goodness—ugly but glorious.

Not one to default to shame, she simply said, "Here it is. Enjoy!"

Quiet at first, we all broke into laughter and began digging in with forks and abandon.

I'd love a handful of that ugly chocolate cake right now.

I loved Mom's over-the-top-ness.

And I loved those rare laughs with Dad.

Living Unhurried

IT WAS SPRING BREAK, just a few months after Scotty and I becam[e] friends. Kristy, the girls, and I were headed south to Florida aga[in] for a few days.

"Have a nice break in Florida," he texted me. "Offer them [an] unhurried, nonanxious spirit. And catch some fish, Russ."

The phrase was new to me: "an unhurried, nonanxious spirit[."]

It reminded me of Paul's words: "Look carefully then how yo[u] walk, not as unwise but as wise, making the best use of the tim[e,] because the days are evil" (Ephesians 5:15-16). Scotty's messag[e] wasn't just a pragmatic "don't waste your time" message; it wa[s] a calling to be wise about time itself. This passage presumes w[e] don't have to be prisoners to time but are empowered to be pre[s]ent in the moment. Even as we learn from the past and prepa[re] for the future, we can make the most of every opportunity.

"Why did you tell me to have an unhurried, non-anxious spiri[t?] Why those words?" I asked Scotty after we got back from our tri[p.]

"Because we're allergic to stillness and contentment," h[e]

replied. "Let's start with Sabbath. Sabbath was celebrated in Eden before sin and brokenness ever entered the world. God rested on the seventh day of Creation—not because he was tired, but as a statement of something far greater. Sabbath declares that we are made for communion, reflection, and connection. Sabbath is a redemptive assault on our penchant for 'performancism.' Sabbath is a way of ordering our lives for relationship with God—setting the pace for the next six days. We start with rest. We cease our striving; then we live, work, and play as unto the Lord."

"I know you rise early in the morning, while it's dark and still. What's important about the quiet?" I asked.

"I need to start my day lingering in the welcoming presence of our Father. I'm just as susceptible as anyone to living a driven life rather than a called life. I begin my day with Sabbath rest, slowly reading the Scriptures, remembering the gospel, and fellowshipping with our Father. Not resting is a recipe for disaster. It might build a huge stock portfolio, but it will bankrupt a heart."

⊙   ⊙   ⊙

Four years ago, Kristy's granddaddy passed away. The family decided to host a reception after the funeral in their backyard, with his garden in sight. About fifty people sat around tables, eating barbecue and talking. At one point I sat next to a woman who was in her sixties. I knew her to be a woman of prayer, one who always gave me something insightful or off the wall to tell Kristy later. So I asked her how she was and what she had been doing.

"I spend the mornings with the Lord," she said. "Every morning."

"Oh, great," I said, thinking how quickly we jumped into spiritual talk. "What does that look like for you?"

"I watch the birds," she said. "I used to put out birdseed, but now the Lord brings the birds to me."

This wasn't really language I would use for birds arriving in someone's yard during the summertime. Her mystical explanation seemed near ludicrous to me, but she was confident in her assessment.

Several years after the woman told me this story, I was sitting on my front porch underneath our huge oak tree, being still. I saw a fat red robin high on a limb of a dogwood tree. I heard a rustling, and there was a mole under the pine straw. Two chipmunks scurried across the driveway toward the English ivy and into the safety of the azalea bushes. Then I noticed a little finch perched on a hidden limb of the bush directly in front of me. It must have been there the entire time, but only now was I aware of it.

The Lord brings the birds to me, I could also say.

I thought about the tortoise in the famed fable. He knows something the hare will never know, because the tortoise sees things the hare will never see. Not only will the hare burn out in exhaustion, since the pace is too fast for the length of the race, but the hare misses the beauty along the way. The hare only wins if he wins, but the tortoise wins even if he loses.

Blaise Pascal, a theologian and mathematician from the seventeenth century, said, "I have discovered that all the unhappiness of men arises from one single fact, that they cannot stay quietly in their own chamber."[2] I began to wonder what good in me and around me, not to mention the good of God, I might grow aware of in the grace of stillness. I began to see how often I fall into the trap of *doing* spirituality rather than *being* with God.

The word meaning "be still" in Psalm 46:10 ("Be still, and know that I am God") means "to sink down; to let go; to become quiet and abandon all." Stillness is a call to abandon all as I worship or read or pray. I think it's a calling, at least for me, to a freer space where quiet and calm can be experienced.

I began to practice stillness in prayer in the mornings when I arrived at my office. I sat in my desk chair, propped my feet on the windowsill, gazed out the window at the treetops, breathed, and grew aware of my thoughts, feelings, and my beloved self.

I gave myself the grace to let go, to sink down, to abandon busy thought.

At first, my thoughts ran wild. To simply breathe and "be" was painful for my frenzied mind. I felt like theologian Gerald May as he journeyed into the "power of slowing." He writes poetically about camping by himself in the wilderness: "My mind still wants to figure things out, still feels it has to be up to something, but it just can't do it. *Settle down, mind. My sweet, good-working, diligent mind, rest awhile. It's okay, really.*"[3]

After my mind calmed and started to let go, my emotions began to surface about stories I thought were in the past but were more present in my current life than ever—narratives that were more dominant drivers than I realized. I felt brokenness, rejection, and sadness. In the power of slowness, with the help of the Holy Spirit, I dared to not move on from the narratives and my emotions. I embraced the revelatory thoughts and feelings and asked them why they'd arisen, opening myself to what God wanted to speak to me.

My cousin Jenn taught me we can be like people standing on the side of a roaring river, watching thoughts and emotions pass by, without being a prisoner to them. We can learn to say, "Look at that; I'm angry. I wonder what that's about." For me, this means I can notice my thoughts and feelings without my thoughts and feelings being completely me. Rather, they're a part of me, worthy of being brought to the Abba Father for confession, healing, and transformation.

● ● ●

"Was your burnout at fifty related to a lack of rest?" I asked Scotty. I knew the outline of what happened but not the details.

"I was preaching four times every Sunday for eight years, and I *loved* it. God was doing remarkable things in downtown Franklin through Christ Community Church. But what I didn't realize was that I was becoming addicted to ministry. It was my 'Christian cocaine.' I allowed the experience of being used *by* the Lord to substitute for spending time *with* him. I was too busy, with no margins, and I was always saying yes. I exhausted myself spiritually, emotionally, mentally, and physically. And then I had nothing left."

"Why were you getting burned out?" I asked.

"Isn't that pretty obvious? I was running from my pain by overworking," he said. "And when your work is ministry, it can be especially seductive and deceptive."

"You were trying to keep the scales tipped toward doing enough?"

"Well, kind of. I didn't necessarily think about it in terms of scales, but more in terms of medicating my pain and dealing with shame. Only the Holy Spirit can enable us to hear our Father say, 'I want you more than what you can do for me.' Through the gospel of God's grace, we can really believe that Jesus didn't come to condemn us but to redeem us. He didn't come to shame us but to heal us, free us, and love us. The things I was doing weren't bad things, but the good became the enemy of the best. Doing things *for* Jesus supplanted walking intimately *with* him. It wasn't simply about getting a better schedule; I needed to become a healthy man."

I'm still trying to figure out how to carry the weight of my work and not be crushed by it. "Either your work is God's, or it is yours," a pastor friend told me bluntly several years ago. I want a quiet heart; I want to be present in the moment. But my busy heart often takes over. I have to listen to the Holy Spirit's whisper that I am God's beloved, or even the gift of stillness and slowness can become a law that will crush me, just another demand.

Scotty's words were as reassuring as they were haunting: a person can be successful and unhealthy.

So as long as we are our broken selves in this broken world, we have to keep reevaluating how we define success.

●　　●　　●

From Scotty
I Was Forty-Nine

It was the summer of 1999, a year before I would gain the courage to open myself up to my daughter. I was still a busy man with a busy heart. Surrounded by tour buses, Kmarts, big churches, and long lines, I was on the *Speechless* tour with Steven Curtis

Chapman. We were on the road promoting his new CD and our book, *Speechless*. I was so proud of the subtitle I'd created for the book: "Living in Awe of God's Disruptive Grace." I had no idea I was prophesying my own future. I suppose I was "clueless" before I was "speechless."

As I was about to experience, God's grace disrupts us and dismantles us before it delights us. It takes us down before it lifts us up, revealing the depth of our need before providing the wonders of God's love. God has a pattern of humbling his children before healing them. He gave Jonah a big-fish experience (see Jonah 1–2); he gave King David a prophet-in-your-face moment (see 2 Samuel 12); and he gave Saul, soon to become Paul, a blinded-from-heaven gift (see Acts 9). He gave me the "blessing" of burnout. Though I don't put myself in the same category as those biblical servants of God, I do believe God loves all his children equally and is heaven-bent on our freedom and peace.

Steven and I were at the end of the *Speechless* tour, having shared new songs and highlights from the book in many venues. We felt comfortable and encouraged. Our last stop was at the Cincinnati Convention Center for a big Youth Specialties event. Steven sang his heart out to a greatly appreciative crowd of several thousand. Then I came onstage, completely ready and relaxed, and opened my mouth. It wasn't stage fright, a senior moment, or a ministroke, but instantly my mind went blank, my mouth felt tacky-dry, and all my oratory skills and tricks vanished.

Friends who were there didn't experience my moment with the same degree of existential crisis I was feeling. They just thought I was off my game, tour-tired, or distracted, but in reality,

I was helpless and powerless. Those twelve minutes onstage felt like twelve months. I'd been running on empty for several years and didn't realize it. My friend Dan's comments about my failure to deal with Mom's death and my frantically busy heart had yet to journey from my mind into my heart.

The adrenaline of a "successful ministry" kept me going the way the next hit for a functioning addict does—for a while. But God, who is rich in mercy, is also creative in his humbling strategies. Burnout has a way of slowing you down—like all the way down to a screeching halt. The warning lights on a car's dashboard are there for a reason. The orange service light is usually a gentle reminder to change the oil and filter. But the red "check engine" light is more foreboding, indicating a major problem. What would you think of a driver who put a piece of masking tape over his brightly lit warning indicator? What would you say about a pastor who tried to mask the obvious signs of burnout in his life?

I came off the stage much more than embarrassed. I was convicted by the Spirit that I was in a dangerous, unhealthy condition. I didn't need to sleep it off; I needed help—big help. Jonah had been ignoring the warning of small waves, so he had to become whale vomit. I had been ignoring God's gentle wooings, but now I couldn't avoid his severe kindness. I was physically fried, mentally spent, spiritually empty, and emotionally fragile. Hallelujah, I finally owned it.

Darlene's prayers had finally met a good ending . . . or rather, a good beginning.

Defining Success

EACH YEAR MY CHURCH graciously gives me a few weeks off in July to find respite from the pressure of studying, preaching, leading, and ministering. It gives my family and me the opportunity to rest and remember why it is we do what we do. When July arrives, I turn my phone off, leave my laptop at home, and leave town for several weeks—whether I want to or not.

It takes several days for me to fully disconnect on a sabbatical. I reach into my pocket for my phone, but my pocket is empty. I feel phantom vibrations from a device that's not with me. I have urges to check my email and write down ideas about everything from sermon series to book concepts to the creation of new programs.

Each day looks the same on sabbatical. I begin by going for a long morning walk, pumping out a hundred push-ups, and then sitting quietly on the porch. On about day four, I finally hear the quiet whisper of the Holy Spirit:

I'm with you now, and I'll be with you when you return home.
Be still.
Don't overcomplicate it.

Last summer, during the third week of sabbatical, we flew to Denver and drove seven hours through the mountains to Telluride, a little town in southwest Colorado. The town is in a box canyon, the walls of the mountains shooting high above the tree line from the old mining town nestled in the valley along the San Miguel River.

One evening Kristy, the girls, and I took the gondola from the old town up to Mountain Village, the ski town built on a ridge above, to eat dinner. On our return, two men shared the gondola with us, and in those close quarters, we began talking. I learned that the older of the two, dressed as if he had a good bit of material wealth, lived with his family in Mountain Village most of the year, when he wasn't taking a break from winter back at his home in California. The younger man, his business partner, was also from California. They wrote software and had sold their first company ten years ago for a sum that made them independently wealthy.

To be honest, this life sounded dreamy to me: waking up each morning to walk in the soaring mountains or ski down the slopes, being autonomous and financially free. We were in the same gondola but also worlds apart. I'd saved money and airline miles the entire year to get my family to this town for one week. When it was over, I had to return to a job. Yet we were both in the same place at the same time.

I thought about Scotty's words: "Success is an unhurried,

nonanxious spirit." True success isn't bound by location, circumstance, or finances. If this is true, then these wealthy men and I can both be successful—and bank accounts, circumstances, decisions, and career trajectory don't add to or take away from that.

◉   ◉   ◉

Perhaps not coincidentally, the conversation I had with Scotty right before leaving for sabbatical was about success.

"Every culture has a narrative about success," he told me. "But the gospel changes how we think about it. Our definition of success will dictate our schedules, our checkbooks, and our relationships with other people."

Scotty shared about his mentor's maxim for success: "My spiritual father, Jack Miller, always quoted Galatians 5:6: 'The only thing that counts is faith expressing itself through love' (NIV). So I now consider success as more about my relationships than about my life stats. I'm not Scotty who weighs in at X salary and Y years in my career and Z books written. Instead, the mark of success is how well I've loved. A life well-lived involves inviting the people around me to taste the goodness and grace of God, to be known and enjoyed. Success is about, *Am I becoming freer to love well, no matter the context?*"

"To love someone is to be present with them?" I asked.

"Yes, but more than just physically present. The gospel enables us to offer people a non-anxious spirit. I enjoy God's peace to the extent that I live with an awareness of his great delight in me through Jesus, and his sovereignty over all things."

Most days I still think the man on the gondola in Telluride has it all. But if I slow myself down, if I stop spending every moment trying to achieve, I see we both have the same opportunity—the present moment. He has different rooms with different views, but we both have the "now."

It is possible to live as frantically in Telluride as we do at home (I should know, because I've done it). The great rescue, greater than an escapist dream, is to stop associating our success with our own accomplishments. Instead, we can give and receive from a posture of grace.

As I began to latch on to this new perspective, I started to say no to breakfast meetings. It might sound like a little thing, but it was big for my daily life. It took years for me to admit it, but I hate breakfast meetings. I always took the invitation out of obligation, and starting the morning in a hurried state set a pace of busyness for the rest of the day. I committed to making the morning an unrushed time so I could wake into quiet before demands and interactions took over.

Sometimes I think we're looking for big chunks of "quiet time"—solid hours set aside for prayer and contemplation. And while it's certainly important to set aside specific time to quiet our hearts, we also need to take advantage of small pockets of quiet throughout our day. These five- or ten-minute windows for space, reading, stillness, prayer, and meditation are available . . . if you give yourself permission to stop the to-do list or the rushing mind. Ten minutes between meetings or appointments. Five minutes before turning on the TV. Fifteen minutes in a parking lot before you are due to enter.

"We are not only freed *from* some things," Scotty told me.

"We are freed *for* other things. The gospel frees us from self-pity to care for others. We are freed from looking to people for our joy so we can find greater joy in knowing Jesus and serving others."

●　　●　　●

After Kristy, the girls, and I returned home from Telluride, I began rising early to start each day writing in the stillness of my home office. In the evenings, after dinner, bedtimes, and tuck-ins, Kristy and I would talk and then watch a show together. She would fall asleep on the couch and eventually head to bed. I would stay up another thirty minutes to enjoy the quiet in our home and the peace of the four human beings I love most as they slept. Before heading to bed, I would walk the dog one last time.

The Georgia heat was slowly giving way to the night, and the cicadas were singing. In the evening stillness, I realized the cicadas could sound like a buzz of annoyance or a song of majesty, depending on my heart's condition—busy or slow.

Success is the same, really. My heart's condition—that is, my remembrance or forgetfulness of who God says I am—makes all the difference.

Resting in Peace

MY FRIEND ED DIED LAST YEAR. He was in his nineties and had been married to Judy for sixty-eight years. He had two children, five grandchildren, and four great-grandchildren. Ed worked for forty years as an aluminum salesman before retiring, buying a farm, and raising and breeding horses along the Tennessee River.

I only knew Ed during his final few years of life, when he and Judy began attending our church. He walked slowly, with a cane, but he always made it down the aisle to receive Communion, flashing me a big smile each time.

I visited him in hospice as his body withered and his breathing slowed. Over the course of several visits, he began slipping away before my eyes. His coughing increased, he stopped speaking, and his ornery sense of humor faded away. I would sit with Judy as she shared their life story, reflecting on the ups and downs.

She kept saying, "We've had a good life."

At first, I sat with Ed because it was my job. But gradually I found that Judy was showing me what it meant to be still in this sacred space. I was learning to simply be with people instead of trying to fix the situation or rushing to the next appointment or item on my to-do list.

Judy called me the day hospice told her that Ed had hours left rather than days. I knew I needed to visit Ed one last time.

As I sat beside him, he was incoherent and in a deep sleep. His head rested to the side.

"Ed, will you tell me about your farm?" I asked, placing my hand on his wrist.

Without hesitation, as if life surged through him one last time, he moved his head upright and opened his eyes. "That was some place," he said with a smile.

"I bet it was," I replied. "Ed, you're going to die soon. I need to ask you if you are at peace with death and with God."

A smirk appeared on his face, revealing his characteristic playfulness. "If he'll have me."

Judy and I laughed lightly. "He'll have you, because Jesus is enough for you," I said, and he nodded in acknowledgement.

"Grace and peace to you, Ed. Go back to sleep, and you just think about your farm."

○   ○   ○

I like to think Ed died walking the pastures along the Tennessee River with his horses grazing around him, the sun shining on his shoulders, and deep rest in his soul.

For someone who is in Christ, death is the ultimate rest for the soul, the ultimate peace from the noise and busyness in this world and in our own hearts. There's nothing slower and more non-anxious than death.

Most days I ignore death, the great inescapable truth awaiting us all. The more I'm attached to dreams in this world, the more anxiety death creates in me. I have so much more I want to do and see, and death calls all of that into question. But being in touch with death redefines what truly matters.

In some ways, Ed's death was easy. He lived a full, long life. He wasn't five or fifteen or thirty-five years old. But we have no say in when our time will come. I want to control death, just as I attempt to control everything else in my life, and yet death will take us all.

I'm going to die. My wife will die. My children will die. Everybody I love will die.

Scotty taught me there is freedom in accepting the inevitable fact that we will all die—and that in Christ, we have *already* passed from death to life. Death is still profoundly sad and worthy of our grief, but ultimately it moves us toward freedom.

The apostle Paul wrote that to be away from the body is to be present with the Lord (see 2 Corinthians 5:8). This means the grave has already been robbed of its victory. Since death ushers us to God, it is the entry to ultimate rest, freedom, and fulfillment. I'm not sure of the details of heaven, but I am sure of the essence: every fear will be gone, and every tear will be wiped away (see Revelation 21:4).

"This image of God tenderly touching our cheek as we weep isn't just as a way for him to relinquish our sadness and fears," Scotty told me. "It's a way to make sense of them."

I can think of no greater rest.

From Scotty
Prayerful Contemplation

1. When you are restless and driven, who experiences the impact most? Who pays the greatest price for your busyness?

2. Would you say your restlessness, hurry, and anxiety are most connected to not having enough, not being enough, or being afraid of missing out? Explain.

3. Scripture calls us to guard our hearts—to nourish, protect, and care for them (see Proverbs 4:23). What might this look like for you in this next season of life? Where do you need to begin?

4. What do you think keeps you from hearing the voice of the Spirit declaring God's great delight in you? Unbelief? Shame? A noisy heart? Not taking the time to listen? Something else?

5. Stewarding our yeses and nos is very much like making wise investments. What do you need to say yes to and no to in order to live more consistently at the "pace of grace"?

NORMAL CAN BE EXTRAORDINARY.

Being Normal

"Is ambition a bad thing?" I asked Scotty one day when I was working hard on my sermon and my writing.

"Having a sense of impact and purpose is a good thing," he said. "But make sure you root those longings in the right story and the right glory. We matter, but we're not the point. I've lived through pastoring a 'Camelot' church . . . and then having Camelot become 'Car-Lot'—having a huge, everybody-wants-to-be-there church, and then watching that same church no longer be the 'church of the first buzz.' It was painful to watch so many people move on to other churches. But the size of our church didn't define me, so it couldn't destroy me. If we define ourselves by the wrong metrics, in time, we will despair—ending life bankrupt of true riches. Only God has the right to define success."

I've learned that having a quiet heart doesn't mean not having dreams. It means our dreams don't define or enslave us. The full gaze of our hearts isn't dependent on them coming true.

Our broader culture has infected Christian subculture with the disease of "success"—the idea that bigger is better, that more is marvelous. We've become insatiable consumers, performers rather than adorers, observers rather than servants. Though God tells us "in quietness and trust is your strength" (Isaiah 30:15, NIV), we often say to him, "in muchness and manyness will we find our meaning."

The prophet Jeremiah wrote to exiles in Babylon who were living in a foreign land,

> Build houses and live in them; plant gardens and eat their produce. Take wives and have sons and daughters; take wives for your sons, and give your daughters in marriage, that they may bear sons and daughters; multiply there, and do not decrease. But seek the welfare of the city where I have sent you into exile, and pray to the LORD on its behalf, for in its welfare you will find your welfare.
> JEREMIAH 29:5-7

Jeremiah's instructions to the Israelites apply to us, too. We are to be extraordinary in the place we reside, as we go about the normal day-to-day functions. Live somewhere. Love that place and those people. Build great marriages and families. Raise and adore your children. Work hard and build community. Drive in traffic and sing. Do the dishes and pray. We often make the mistake of thinking that being extraordinary means you have to be the next Mother Teresa or Bill Gates or Martin Luther King Jr. You don't have to change the world by being on the grand stages of society. We are called into a Kingdom where God is changing the world and welcomes us to be participants, whether we dance on stages or befriend someone in our cul-de-sac. When we live out radical love in our normal lives, that's when grace turns everything upside down.

●　　●　　●

Almost twenty years ago, when I was at L'Abri, I took a day off from my studies and rode a train into London to spend time with friends who were on study-abroad programs in the city. We toured the historic sites and shopped at the charming market in Notting Hill. Late in the day we decided to attend a musical, so I didn't board a train for the two-hour return ride south until past dark.

I passed the time on the train reading and thinking about what I would do with my life.

Which seminary should I attend?
What kind of job will I get?
How will I launch myself into the world after college?
Will I get married, and when? To whom?

These questions of my future came with both hope and fear.

When the train stopped in the village of Greatham, I deboarded and began the two-mile walk to the manor home. It was April, and the cutting wind of winter had turned to a mild, crisp breeze. There were a few streetlights spread out along the two-lane country road, but for the most part I walked in darkness, lit only by a thousand radiant stars. The lone sound was the loose gravel crunching on the asphalt as I walked down the middle of the road.

After walking for about a mile, I could see neither the train station I'd left nor the crossroad I would turn at, and I stopped to look up at the stars. I knew the stars were galaxies away, but they felt near. As I stared at them, the distance between us grew smaller, and suddenly a wave of fear overcame me.

No one was there, but there was a Presence.

I was certain of it.

I was on the other side of the world, far from friends and family, in the middle of nowhere. This was twenty years ago, so there was no phone in my pocket. Nobody in the world knew where I was in that moment, and it was both terrifying and freeing. I thought about running. I was a fast runner, but for some reason, my feet didn't move. I grew aware that the Presence wasn't there to shame me but to be with me, to be my mighty fortress against all the fear, shame, and sin rumbling in my heart.

Then the Spirit spoke to my spirit,

> *I know exactly where you are.*
> *I know exactly who you are.*
> *I know all of you, and I love all of you.*

In that moment I was terrified, as I wasn't yet ready to be fully known. I couldn't have articulated it at the time, but I wasn't sure I wanted to know myself.

> *What if I wasn't good enough?*
> *What if I was normal?*

Francis Schaeffer, the theologian who founded L'Abri, writes, "We all tend to emphasize big works and big places, but all such emphasis is of the flesh. To think in such terms is simply to hearken back to the old, unconverted, egoist, self-centered *Me*. This attitude, taken from the world, is more dangerous to the Christian than fleshly amusement or practice. It is the flesh."[1] Schaeffer goes on to say that Christians should proactively seek the lowest position, even as we're tempted to look for greater positions of prestige.

In the little places, where there is less pressure, we can more easily practice drawing close to God and resting in him. And then if God opens the doors to positions of increased responsibility and influence, we can move forward already equipped in humility, gratitude, and quietness. When we step out of the spotlight, away from accolades and attention, we learn to take comfort in the Lord rather than in our own power or performance. As Scotty says, "Seek to live with gospel astonishment wherever God places you."

The world wants to speed us up, but our heavenly Father is committed to slowing us down. Too many churches tend to communicate, "Get busy and show God you're sincere." But our Father says, "Be still, and know that I am God" (Psalm 46:10). We aren't to give God bit parts in our stories. We are to live as characters in and carriers of his Story.

◎   ◎   ◎

"What does it mean for someone to be extraordinary?" I asked Scotty. I was struggling with the tension between ambition and calling.

How could I know whether my efforts were driven by performance or love?

"As I near the last chapter of my life, I relish more quiet. I relish contentment," Scotty said. "Those are the places I find satisfaction for my soul. I want to feast on the bread of grace and the manna of acceptance. We can waste our lives trying to build another Tower of Babel, or we can rightfully invest our lives in the unshakable Kingdom of God. If we're ever going to find peace and rest, we have to settle into a primary state of being with Jesus, not doing things for Jesus. He's the one making all things new, including us. That is an extraordinary life, no matter what it looks like in the eyes of the world."

In the 1500s, theologian and reformer Martin Luther was approached by a cobbler who had become a Christian.

He asked Luther, "What should I do now?" At the time, clergy often taught (unbiblically) that contemplative work was of a higher order than manual labor. Implicit in the man's question was the idea, *Certainly, I can't remain a cobbler*.

To the man's surprise, Luther responded, "Then make a good shoe and sell it at a fair price."[2]

Luther realized that being a Christian doesn't always move someone from being a cobbler to a clergy member but rather transforms a person's heart and motives in their daily life. This idea became known as the doctrine of vocation, which calls us to love our neighbor through our everyday work. This means that spirituality is available to everyone, not just those who do certain kinds of work.

As we read the Creation story, it's important to note that work was not a result of the Fall. Adam and Eve worked in a perfected state before they sinned. They tended a garden and found joy in doing it well. And while our work has been affected by this broken world, it has also been redeemed by the gospel. That means you aren't just making a shoe. You're making a shoe someone will wear, and that act brings beauty and kindness and order to the world.

In the past couple of years, two fears have surfaced in my heart and mind. I fear my work will not go well by the standards of the world and my own fleshly standards of greatness, and I will come to the conclusion that I am not enough or that my work was in vain. My second fear is that my work will go unimaginably well and that even then I will still end up feeling inadequate; I will still be searching for meaning.

I shared these fears with Scotty, and he didn't bat an eye.

"Of course you feel that way," he said, offering neither judgment nor advice.

He knew I already knew where my soul must rest.

Loving Others

DARLENE AND SCOTTY'S MOVE to Nashville from Winston-Salem, North Carolina, in 1979 was quite disruptive for their family. Darlene was pregnant at the time and wasn't crazy about the move. But God does some of his best grace-work in our disruptions and transitions, and this proved true for Darlene. This is when she started working with a counselor whom God used greatly, freeing Darlene to grieve parts of her story she'd never voiced, processed, or wrestled with in the presence of our Father.

Darlene loved Scotty well by resisting the temptation to try to fix him or goad him into counseling. She lived in the painful tension of wanting more for him and their marriage while remaining committed to processing her own childhood trauma and deep heart wounds. She watched God use Scotty in great ways but grieved over how shut down his heart had become. He was much more engaged in the pulpit than he was with her heart.

Henri Nouwen explains how this type of judgment-free love is possible: "Can we free ourselves from the need to judge others? Yes, by claiming for ourselves the truth that we are the Beloved daughters and sons of God."[3] Nouwen writes that as long as we are held in bondage to what we do, what we have, and what other people think of us, we will continue to judge others and ourselves. It's only when we embrace the truth of our identity as God's beloved that we can let go of our need to judge.

In 1 John 3:1, we are told to behold the lavish love of God. Once we understand that God loves us and that God is love, we are able to love others (see 1 John 4:7-8). John writes about our position of belovedness while calling us into mission. The mission to love is never without love from God to our souls, or else mission becomes law, which in time always condemns and exhausts us. But when mission is driven by God's grace and flows from our belovedness, it creates true regard for others. That means we no longer have to judge someone else to feel better about ourselves.

In love, all our judgment is transformed into compassion.

When you love someone, you run into their faults, just as they run into yours. The difficulty is to love someone without trying to fix them. Scotty says that loving others becomes more of the flow of grace when we simply trust that God is God. We know he is at work, so we can be with others without needing to change them or impress them. We can simply be with them. The pace of grace is to live, work, and play alongside people in the ordinary moments.

From the position of our secure identity flows nonjudgmental love and forgiveness toward all people in all places. We become reconcilers in this world, taking a position of humility in relationships, even while maintaining wisdom and self-care. This path is not easy, but it is the call to radical love. We aren't called to be forgetful or without boundaries, but to be shockingly gracious and forgiving toward each other.

Desmond Tutu, the theologian and clergyman known for his work for human rights and anti-apartheid in South Africa, says, "Forgiveness is taking seriously the awfulness of what has happened when you are treated unfairly. . . . Forgiveness is not pretending that things are other than they are."[4] Forgiveness means releasing the person who owes you something—and releasing your desire for vengeance upon them—while still recognizing the horror done and the woundedness experienced. Because our own sins have been forgiven completely, we are inspired to risk forgiveness too.

For much of my life, I wanted to fix other people, to mold them into who I deemed they should be. I wanted control. But as I let go of trying to fix people, I find the freedom to be present with them and the gracious space to love and enjoy them.

When we love this way, we can live with imperfect people, porcupine quills and all.

◎　　◎　　◎

From Scotty
At Mom's Grave

It was February of 2000, nearly forty years after I rode in a big, black car as an eleven-year-old boy, newly motherless, to a hole in the ground that would soon consume my mom's body. I hadn't been back since.

But my burnout changed everything. I was at the end of myself. Dan's words and Darlene's kindness and the faithfulness of God allowed my burnout to become a portal to hope. The road of healing I was on led straight to Alamance Memorial Park.

Some car rides seem to take forever because of how badly we want to get to our destination. When I was a kid, the four-hour ride to the beach felt like fourteen. But other trips, like this drive to the cemetery, seem too short because we dread arriving.

Darlene was under my arm, and we walked the fifteen yards from our car to the grave marker I'd never read.

Martha Ward Smith
September 10, 1923–October 10, 1961

Mom was barely thirty-eight years old when the head-on crash ripped her from my life. Nothing had defined me more than the impact of her death. Standing over Mom's grave, my heart dam was breached. Grief flooded me, and I wept tears that had been bottled up inside for nearly four decades.

Some dams need to break. The wait was over, and the weight of grace began to flood my heart.

Rather than providing closure, going to the grave served as an opening for me. I had lived for forty years in complete avoidance, trying to stuff down my memories of Mom. That changed after my visit to her grave. I put up one of my favorite photos of Mom on the table right beside my bed. I began to allow myself to remember her laugh, her smell, and her touch. I wish I could remember more, but I relish anything I'm given.

Acknowledging the trauma of my mom's death allowed me to look at other parts of my story—my abuse, my busy heart, and my relationships with those I love the most. Just days after I wept at Mom's grave, I looked at Darlene and said, "Honey, I'm ready to go to counseling with you."

With those words, Darlene and I started a journey that continues to this day. In the summer of 2000, our counselor sent us to a ten-day counseling intensive on the West Coast. It was one of the most painfully fruitful experiences in our marriage—one that plowed the fields of our souls and prepared us for the heart work ahead.

Redemption, I was learning, is less about getting over hard things and more about growing through them.

Finding Contentment

When Scotty's dad was in his mideighties, he began to slip into dementia. Paranoia and suspicion did not take over for him, as it does with many. Instead, he grew kinder and began to communicate with Scotty in ways he never had before. Even as he forgot Scotty's name and eventually his face, he became more tender. It wasn't unusual for him to break into spontaneous singing, and he began to recall stories from his childhood.

"He was a bad man," he said to Scotty one day. "He was evil."

"Who are you talking about, Dad?"

"He really hurt my mother—your grandmother," he said. "I remember my mother, my siblings, and me not having shoes on our feet. But my father always had money to take his friends drinking. One day he got drunk and broke my arm."

Until his dad's dementia blew off boundaries and restraint, Scotty didn't know the abuse and pain his dad had endured as a kid and young man. That explained his dad's rush to leave home and join the Navy. It explained his dad's rigid, controlling heart. It explained so much.

The evil and abuse Scotty's dad experienced never entered Scotty's home life, but the trauma he endured made it difficult for him to connect with Scotty and his brother. It was as if Scotty's dad had the heart space to love one person deeply, and that was Scotty's mom. The grief that filled his dad's heart never faded, and he lived a life with little peace, little contentment.

"Contentment and compassion are linked," Scotty explained to me. "Being discontented means we have limited capacity to empathize with and love others." But when we know we are beloved, when we are at home in our identity in Christ, we can see the person in front of us without needing them to make us content.

Paul wrote to the Philippians about what contentment looks like. This takes on added significance knowing he wrote these words when he was imprisoned:

> Not that I am speaking of being in need, for I have
> learned in whatever situation I am to be content. I know
> how to be brought low, and I know how to abound. In
> any and every circumstance, I have learned the secret of
> facing plenty and hunger, abundance and need. I can do
> all things through him who strengthens me.
> PHILIPPIANS 4:11-13

In high school I had a poster in my basketball locker of a famous Christian athlete with that last verse plastered across it: "I can do all things through him who strengthens me." It turns out the verse has nothing to do with empowering me to dunk but something to say to my soul in all my successes and failures. I've come to understand contentment as being satisfied with one's lot, independent of external circumstances.

●　　●　　●

When our church first moved into the building we currently occupy—which had been an old textile warehouse and then a data center before sitting vacant for several years—we finished the children's classrooms but had only a big, bare room for our sanctuary until we raised the capital to build a better-equipped space. After saving money for another three years, we added on space for a new sanctuary. The first Sunday after we moved into the space, I stayed after to read in my office for a couple of hours to get a head start on the next week's sermon. Everyone else had left, and the building was empty. I walked from my office down the long corridor toward the kitchen. The building and the new sanctuary made things feel more stable, but I knew better.

True stability is an issue of the heart.

People will come and go from our church, and we will rejoice and we will be sad. Our church may grow, plateau, or even shrink in size, and I won't hold ultimate control. All of life, not just my work, is more fragile than I realize—and requires trust. Stable joy will always be found only in the Lord.

By the time I got to the end of the corridor, light was spilling in from the courtyard garden. As I looked into the new sanctuary, my heart was filled with gratitude for the people who gave and served and came to receive in this place. I headed to the side of the sanctuary into an unlit section of the building where there was no natural light.

I didn't reach for the light switch; I knew these halls by heart. I walked into the darkness, and I was taken back to the figurative darkness I'd encountered when we started the church and my interior life felt like it was about to crumble. I was reminded of the parts of my heart even now that fall prey to anxiety and fear. But as I walked through the dark hallway, my eyes adjusted, and I was overcome with a sense of Presence.

My mind flashed back to our first month of Sunday morning services, when we were meeting in the preschool. I was waking up in the middle of the night then, wondering how to keep everything going, afraid I would fall apart. One Sunday, after setting out the seventy-five chairs, putting together the Communion table, and hauling in the pulpit, I sat in the middle of the preschool auditorium, the walls covered in primary colors and children's artwork.

A friend who had helped start the church came and sat next to me. He leaned over and said, "If this is all it ever is, this is great."

I wish I'd believed him at the time. I see now this is all it ever is, and this is great. I wish I'd believed many things and put greater trust in God rather than myself along the way. I wish I weren't my own worst enemy when it comes to joy and peace. Scotty says this is normal; it's part of learning contentment now and also longing for a day in eternity when the sweat, the weeds, and the tears will be no more.

Comedian and actor Jim Carrey says, "I think everybody should get rich and famous and do everything they ever dreamed of so they can see that it's not the answer."[5] I once heard another comedian say, "If you aren't happy on the plane, you won't be happy in Hawaii."

No matter what we achieve, no matter what people think of us, we are always the same souls needing God's tenacious grace to carry us along.

We will never find contentment if we buy into the "arrival fallacy," the idea that gratification will come at some future point after we've achieved a certain status, accomplishment, or relationship. The arrival fallacy promotes the futility of the performance-driven life—always moving, buying, earning, but never really arriving.

Always somewhere, but never where we want to be.

And never at peace.

The gospel is the antidote to the arrival fallacy.

Christ's love, his work for us, and his presence with us—these are sufficient. This moment holds meaning, joy, and peace. Even as we long for eternity, here and now is enough.

Our stories of fluctuating between anxiety and contentment will one day end. And just as the lamb and the wolf will lie down together (see Isaiah 11:6), our love and our fear will be reconciled.

○　　○　　○

From Scotty
My Conversation with Dad

It was ten days after Darlene and I visited Mom's grave.

It had been thirty-nine years since Dad and I had spoken of Mom.

I was fifty, and Dad was eighty-one.

The week after Darlene and I returned home from visiting Mom's grave in Burlington, Dad called to announce that he and Ruth, my stepmom, were coming for a visit. His call irritated me at first. He never asked; he just announced. And I was still reeling from the impact of my visit to Mom's grave.

But it made all the sense in the world to Darlene. She'd been praying and waiting for healing and reconciliation between my dad and me. Of course God would bring Dad to me. (I certainly didn't have a track record of initiating anything with him.) It was much easier to do life side by side than to risk breaking equilibrium in a face-to-face relationship.

With Darlene's encouragement, I asked Dad to go with me to McDonald's the morning after he and Ruth arrived. I'd driven by the Brentwood, Tennessee, McDonald's dozens of times but never stopped until this mid-February Tuesday. I knew it was time to risk making my way into Dad's world.

Dad was thrilled by the invitation because at least five days a week, that's how he began his day in Burlington—standing outside McDonald's at five till five waiting for the doors to open. Though my dad could have bought a McDonald's franchise or two, he embraced the privileges he assumed went with being a senior citizen. Whenever he crossed under the welcome of the Golden Arches, Dad usually took a well-used McDonald's coffee cup with him for free refills. He also had a habit of bringing an apple to eat after his Egg McMuffin. "Why spend money if you don't have to?" was his forever mantra.

With two Egg McMuffins and cups of coffee in hand (my

treat—no free refill this time), Dad and I sat knee-to-knee in a two-man booth. Up until now, I was used to the arrangement of distance. I'd worked to protect it. It kept me safe from the possibility of being rejected by him. I'd sooner expect him to transform into Elvis than to open his heart to me.

Tucked away in my *USA Today* sports section, I had a picture of my mom. After our normal banter around the safe topics of weather, taxes, and sports, I reached for the photo. With my heart racing and my legs crossed out of actual fear I might pee myself, I placed the picture on the table where he could see it. I launched right in. "Dad, I've been meaning to ask you about this picture. What can you tell me about this car?"

It was a five-by-seven black-and-white photo of Mom, Dad, Moose, and me standing around a 1957 Packard automobile. To my surprise, Dad didn't miss a beat. "That's your uncle Max's car—one he fixed up for drag racing. You know how much he loved fast cars."

Though the car occupied 75 percent of the photo, Mom's smile was the most obvious feature. It was the first time since 1961 I could remember gazing at any image of Mom and Dad together.

So far so good, I thought as I pulled out a second picture. "What can you tell me about this one?" It was a picture of the day Mom and Dad were married. He was dressed handsomely in his Merchant Marine officer's uniform. Mom, on his arm, was looking up at Dad with all the excitement of a brand-new bride.

I paused. Dare I make eye contact with Dad? Three seconds felt like three minutes.

Then he spoke. "Scott, that's the day your mom and I got

married." He didn't say her name, Martha—the name I hadn't heard him utter for almost forty years.

For the next ten minutes, Dad gave me a legacy, an inheritance, and finally his still-broken heart. He shared story after story of how the next three weeks unfolded, right after that wedding-day picture was snapped. They honeymooned in New York City, on the government's tab, because Dad was in gyrocompass training as a navigator. With concerts at night and hours to play, they christened and celebrated their new marriage.

"We were in the Brooklyn train station the day I had to send your mom back to Burlington and catch my own train for Los Angeles. That's where I had to board a ship for my next tour of duty," he said.

All of a sudden, Dad went from telling stories from the past to engaging in the moment he had to tell Mom goodbye. "Martha was standing at the top of the stairwell in the train station . . ." He couldn't finish the sentence.

Tears welled up and streamed down his eighty-one-year-old face. I knew the goodbye in New York reminded him of the fierce goodbye we'd both said to Mom four decades earlier. He didn't get up from the booth. He didn't try to regather himself. He wasn't embarrassed. He was free. I reached across the booth and started patting my father on the shoulder as he bent forward and cradled his face.

The physical touch we shared in that moment was a symbol of a long overdue connection. Until that cold February Tuesday, we'd never wept together, rarely touched, and never talked about the greatest love and biggest loss in our lives.

I, too, was being set free in that McDonald's booth, which was somehow transformed into a cathedral of grace. It was the beginning of a relationship that grew with my dad the rest of his healthy days, into his dementia, and until his death.

From Scotty

Prayerful Contemplation

1. The Bible calls contentment "great gain" (1 Timothy 6:6). We usually think the opposite—that we'll only be content after gaining a lot. What circumstances or challenges is God using in your life to slow you down and lead you to reevaluate your priorities?

2. Knowing what you know now, how would you define success differently than you would have five or ten years ago?

3. In what ways can "muchness" and "manyness" lead us to forfeit our souls—to live heartless, soulless, empty lives?

4. Do you have friends who reflect God's grace and truth to you? Do you connect with friends consistently on a heart level? Who do you need to start spending more time with (and less time with) to foster these kinds of relationships?

5. Finish this sentence: "Before I die, I want to . . ." What would it look like for you to take the next step toward making this happen?

6. God's name is Redeemer, not Redo. What would it take for you to enjoy more of God's peace, kindness, and love? (The gospel puts an end to all earning but not all effort.)

7. What does a healthier and freer you look like?

Epilogue

The Last Conversation

I KNEW THE STORY. I knew the heartache, hurt, rejection, redemption, and reconciliation in Scotty's life, and I knew how everything had turned out. But I couldn't shake the vast, looming fear that comes with taking risk after risk, as Scotty did.

I know there are people who have tried this same act of risking for love and were met with their greatest fear when once again they were shut out and shut down, or maybe even worse, met with apathy.

So I had to ask, "But what if your dad had rejected you again?"

"There was no guarantee," Scotty said. "I had to trust I was already beloved."

"I mean, there are a lot of people who walk into a McDonald's to have that conversation and don't receive the same outcome you received."

"Absolutely. Those who live as God's beloved are not always on a trajectory of 'they lived happily ever after,'" Scotty said.

"So you needed that conversation no matter what?"

"That's the difference between pragmatism and grace," Scotty said. "We don't do the next gospel thing to get an intended result. We do the next gospel thing because we are loved. *We are loved.* By the God of the universe. Therefore, we move in love. The next gospel thing for me was to speak with my dad, to move toward him in kindness, with no guarantee of the outcome."

"What gave you the bravery to do it?" I asked.

"It's everything we talk about, Russ. We live under illusions. 'Oh, I can't go there; I can't face that.' But the grace of God is limitless and tenacious. God is for us, and he is faithful. No matter how long we fight or how quickly we learn to rest in it, the grace of God will carry us along, and it's an amazing story for our souls to get caught up in."

◦   ◦   ◦

This education in the grace and peace of God has no graduation. I'll call Scotty, and he'll call me back. We talk as he walks around his neighborhood. Yesterday he texted me a picture of a rainbow trout he caught.

I'll see him soon, I'm sure. He'll tell me "gospel bombs," as he calls them:

You can know the lyric of the gospel but not hear the music.
God wants *us* more than what we can do for him.

Those are my favorites.

Scotty and I still talk about the difficulty and treasure of being a good dad, husband, son, pastor, neighbor, and friend. We converse. We share. We laugh.

It's relationship.

You see, there has always been an eighth lesson: *the relationship itself.*

Knowing and being known.

Loving and being loved.

Notes

THE PORCH CONVERSATION

1. Jackson Browne, "Running on Empty," *Running on Empty*, Asylum, 1977.

THE FIRST CONVERSATION

1. Anne Lamott, *Plan B: Further Thoughts on Faith* (New York: Riverhead Books, 2006), 304.
2. Charles H. Spurgeon, "Taking Possession of Our Inheritance," Sermon #2086 (Metropolitan Tabernacle, Newington, England, May 12, 1889).
3. C. S. Lewis, *The Weight of Glory* (New York: HarperCollins, 2001), 46.
4. Richard Rohr, "Trinity: MIA" (May 5, 2019), Center for Action and Contemplation, https://cac.org/trinity-mia-2019-05-05/.
5. *Gaga by Gaultier*, directed by Alex Fighter and Julie Gali (Paris, France: Dak Tirak Productions, 2011).
6. *Gaga: Five Foot Two*, directed by Chris Moukarbel (Live Nation Productions, Mermaid Films, and Permanent Wave, 2017).
7. Henri J. M. Nouwen, *Life of the Beloved: Spiritual Living in a Secular World* (New York: Crossroad, 2002), 31, 33.
8. "Glossary: *Incurvatus in Se*," Mockingbird, accessed August 13, 2020, https://mbird.com/glossary/incurvatus-in-se/.
9. Crispin Sartwell, "What's So Good about Original Sin?" *New York Times*, May 21, 2018, https://www.nytimes.com/2018/05/21/opinion/original-sin-ethics.html.
10. In God's grace, I was confronted with my internal toxic practice of scorekeeping at the 2011 Birmingham Mockingbird Conference. Paul

Walker delivered a life-changing message entitled "Why We Always Lose When We Keep Score" (Birmingham, AL, October 28, 2011), https://mbird.com/ct_sermon/why-we-always-lose-when-we-keep-score/.

11. The teachings and writings of Ray Cortese, Tim Keller, Paul Walker, Scotty Smith, Steve Brown, and Mockingbird Ministries (notably David Zahl and his father, Paul Zahl) led me to understand the fullness of my absolution and righteousness in Christ.

THE SECOND CONVERSATION

1. Brennan Manning, *Abba's Child: The Cry of the Heart for Intimate Belonging* (Colorado Springs: NavPress, 2015), 42.

2. Henri J. M. Nouwen, *The Only Necessary Thing: Living a Prayerful Life* (New York: Crossroad, 1999), 206.

3. *The Shawshank Redemption*, directed by Frank Darabont (Castle Rock Entertainment, 1994).

4. Dan Barber, "Poultry Slam 2011," interview by Ira Glass, December 2, 2011, in *This American Life*, podcast, 35:47, https://www.thisamericanlife .org/452/poultry-slam-2011.

5. My growing understanding of covenants in the Scriptures is largely thanks to the sermons of Tim Keller, particularly a sermon entitled "A Covenant Relationship," September 9, 2007, Gospel in Life, MP3 audio, 31:29, https://gospelinlife.com/downloads/a-covenant-relationship-5548/.

6. Frederick Buechner, *Whistling in the Dark: A Doubter's Dictionary* (New York: HarperCollins, 1993), 113.

7. L. Frank Baum, *The Wonderful Wizard of Oz* (Chicago, New York, 1900), chap. 16.

THE THIRD CONVERSATION

1. My understanding of parables has been greatly aided by Robert Farrar Capon, *Kingdom, Grace, Judgment: Paradox, Outrage, and Vindication in the Parables of Jesus* (Grand Rapids, MI: Eerdmans, 2002).

THE FOURTH CONVERSATION

1. R.E.M., "Everybody Hurts," *Automatic for the People*, Warner Bros. Records, 1992.

2. Stephen Colbert, interview by Anderson Cooper, "Stephen Colbert on Overcoming Grief and Loss as a Child," *Anderson Cooper 360*, CNN,

August 15, 2019, video, 21:13, https://www.youtube.com/watch?feature
=youtu.be&v=YB46h1koicQ&app=desktop.

THE FIFTH CONVERSATION

1. Vivek H. Murthy, quoted at Hannah Schulze, "Loneliness: An Epidemic?"
   Science in the News (blog), Harvard Graduate School of Arts and Sciences,
   April 16, 2018, http://sitn.hms.harvard.edu/flash/2018/loneliness-an
   -epidemic/.
2. Arthur Schopenhauer, quoted at Walter Veit, "The Hedgehog's
   Dilemma," *Science and Philosophy* (blog), *Psychology Today*, March 28,
   2020, https://www.psychologytoday.com/us/blog/science-and
   -philosophy/202003/the-hedgehog-s-dilemma. See Arthur
   Schopenhauer, *Parerga and Paralipomena: Short Philosophical Essays*,
   trans. E. F. J. Payne, vol. 2 (Oxford: Clarendon, 1974), 651.
3. C. S. Lewis, *The Four Loves* (New York: Harcourt Brace Jovanovich,
   1960), 169–70.
4. Brené Brown, *Daring Greatly: How the Courage to Be Vulnerable
   Transforms the Way We Live, Love, Parent, and Lead* (New York: Penguin,
   2012), 34.
5. J. I. Packer, *Knowing God* (Downers Grove, IL: InterVarsity, 1973), 41–42.
6. Anne Lamott, "Anne Lamott: 'Look at the Tea Party: Some of the
   Angriest, Most Hateful People on Earth, and They're Backed by What
   They Think Is Scripture,'" Salon, December 3, 2014, https://www.salon
   .com/2014/12/03/anne_lamott_look_at_the_tea_party_some_of_the
   _angriest_most_hateful_people_on_earth_and_they%E2%80%99re
   _backed_by_what_they_think_is_scripture/.
7. Brené Brown, *The Gifts of Imperfection: Let Go of Who You Think You're
   Supposed to Be and Embrace Who You Are* (Center City, MN: Hazelden,
   2010), 26.

THE SIXTH CONVERSATION

1. Richard A. Swenson, *Margin: Restoring Emotional, Physical, Financial, and
   Time Reserves to Overloaded Lives* (Colorado Springs: NavPress, 2004), 27.
2. Blaise Pascal, *Pensées*, number 139.
3. Gerald G. May, *The Wisdom of Wilderness: Experiencing the Healing
   Power of Nature* (New York: HarperCollins, 2006), 41.

THE SEVENTH CONVERSATION

1. Francis A. Schaeffer, *No Little People* (Wheaton, IL: Crossway, 2003), 26.
2. Tom Heetderks, *Work Worth Doing: Finding God's Direction and Purpose in Your Career* (Eugene, OR: Harvest House, 2020), 60. This is a secondary source for this story, which has been told and written about for years.
3. Henri J. M. Nouwen, *Here and Now: Living in the Spirit* (New York: Crossroad, 1994), 81.
4. Desmond Tutu, foreword to *Exploring Forgiveness*, eds. Robert D. Enright and Joanna North (Madison: University of Wisconsin Press, 1998), xiii.
5. Jim Carrey, "Quotable Quotes," *Reader's Digest* (March 2006), 81.

Acknowledgments

From Russ

TO MY WIFE, KRISTY: you continually encouraged me and never once complained when I disappeared from our family for a few hours of writing or revisions. My heart is filled with gratitude for who you are and how you love me.

To my daughters: you have softened my heart and taught me playfulness. May this book find a home in you along your journey.

To Mom, Sherry, and all of my family: your support never wavers. You gave me the values of education and persistence. You continue to believe I can somehow start and finish projects like this book.

To my gospel posse friends: our dinners, trips, and texts are refuge for me.

To my friend Owen: your early-on business advice was timely.

To my friends Brad, Bryan, Mary, and Linda: you read a rough draft of the first chapters; thank you for reading such rough beginnings and giving your wisdom.

To my cousin Kate: you always check in on me and this project. It means a lot.

To Jennifer Foushee: you gave endless hours of mind and

heart to read, edit, and proof, helping craft my words and ideas. Thank you for lending me your gifts of writing and editing.

To Laura Lisle: you listened to hours of taped conversations and transcribed them wonderfully.

To WordServe Literary and Keely Boeving: you refined our proposal into something to warrant a book. Thank you for guiding us and introducing us to Tyndale.

To Jon Farrar: you took a proposal and helped us form a book. Early in the process, you said this book would require more of my heart and then it would write itself. You were right.

To Stephanie Rische: you edited with expertise, wisdom, clarity, and grace. You gently pushed us to craft more and better. Along the way, you made this better.

To the team at Tyndale: you put in hours of work behind the scenes to turn a Word document into a book and to place it before readers. Thank you.

To the leaders and people of the Church of the Apostles: a portion of my heart will always live in your church. I'm grateful for the years of love and development my entire family received from you.

To the leaders and people of Christ the Redeemer Church of Marietta: I couldn't have dreamed of a more generous and gracious people to live among and pastor.

To Mockingbird Ministries: your ongoing pursuit to communicate the message of grace in a world of demand has transformed my life and revolutionized my work.

To Mitch Albom and Morrie Schwartz: I read your book, *Tuesdays with Morrie*, twenty years ago and found my heart longing for such a loving mentoring relationship. Without your book, the understanding of what a mentor could be may never have existed inside me. The idea to write about it probably wouldn't have existed either. Your relationship and book continue to be the gold standard.

To Scotty: thank you for saying yes.

About the Authors

Scotty Smith, a native of Graham, North Carolina, is a graduate of the University of North Carolina, Westminster Theological Seminary, and Covenant Theological Seminary (DMin). After planting and pastoring Christ Community Church in Franklin, Tennessee, for twenty-six years, Scotty assumed a position on the pastoral staff of West End Community Church as teacher in residence. He also serves as adjunct faculty for Covenant Seminary, Westminster Theological Seminary (Philadelphia), Reformed Theological Seminary (Orlando), and Western Seminary in Portland, Oregon. Scotty has authored ten books, including *Unveiled Hope* (with Michael Card), *Objects of His Affection*, *Restoring Broken Things* (with Steven Curtis Chapman), *Everyday Prayers: 365 Days to a Gospel-Centered Faith*, and *Every Season Prayers: Gospel-Centered Prayers for the Whole of Life*. Scotty invests time mentoring leaders in many different contexts. He is a coach, a consultant, and an encourager among leaders at AdventHealth/Centra Care in Orlando and with BCW in Dallas—a major wheat and food product supplier. Among his hobbies, Scotty enjoys photography, fishing, cooking, and exercise. Scotty and his wife of almost fifty years, Darlene, live in Franklin, Tennessee. Darlene has two master's degrees from Covenant Seminary, including one in counseling. She has a huge mercy gift, a great laugh, and a big heart, and loves being a grandmother (DeDe) to Finn, Otis, and Otto, and is looking forward to the arrival of a first granddaughter. Scotty's blog, *Heavenward*, is hosted on the Gospel Coalition, and you can follow him on Twitter @ScottyWardSmith.

Russ Masterson is the founding and senior pastor of Christ the Redeemer Church of Marietta. Russ served as a student pastor and a college and singles' pastor before starting Redeemer Marietta. By God's goodness, the church has grown from three families to more than 350 people in seven years. Russ holds degrees from the University of Georgia and New Orleans Baptist Theological Seminary. He is the author of several books, including a memoir, *40 Days without Food*, and a novel, *Adao's Dance*. The past fifteen years of Russ's life have been filled with weekly study and teaching God's one-way love to us in Jesus—grace without any conditions—which frees, heals, and empowers growth in grace. His company, JIG House (JigHouse.com), equips leaders with greater resilience, effectiveness, and well-being; helps them build their teams and make more informed hiring decisions; and empowers them to develop healthy patterns for leadership and life. Russ lives in Marietta with his wife, three daughters, and a joyful labradoodle named Brother.

RussMasterson.cc
TWITTER: RussMasterson
INSTAGRAM: Russ_Masterson
FACEBOOK: RussTMasterson

WORK WITH RUSS

JIG
HOUSE

Russ's company, JIG House, exists to walk leaders toward greater wholeness of the soul, more informed decision making for hiring and team building, and the development of peaceful patterns for leadership and life.

JIG House is a coaching and assessment company. Our offerings serve leaders for the healing and development of their souls, their leadership, and their teams.

Anxiety, pressure, regret, fear, and shame do not have to define us or govern our leadership. We exist to help leaders and teams grow in soul care so they can become more peace filled, loving, and effective at work, family, and play.

You do not have to be alone in this.
www.jighouse.com